Sex,

Intimacy and

Aged Care

BARBARA SHERMAN

This item is made available by Alzheimer's Australia NSW
through the support of the Wentworth Community
Development Support Expenditure Committee and Wentworth
Services Sporting Club . 2004.

For Information, Support and Education
Call the Dementia Helpline 1800 639 331
Website: www.alzheimers.org.au

For Jennah, Melinda, Christopher and Katie

First published 1998
by The Australian Council for Educational Research Ltd
19 Prospect Hill Road, Camberwell, Melbourne, Victoria, 3124

Edited by Brigid James of Writers Reign
Designed and formatted by Lynn Twelftree
Cover designed by Tracey Roberts
Cover illustration by Ursula Kolbe
Printed by Shannon Books

National Library of Australia Cataloguing-in-Publication Data:

Barbara Sherman
  Sex, intimacy and aged care.

  Bibliography.
  Includes index.
  ISBN 0 86431 294 6.

  1. Aged – Sexual behavior. 2. Dementia – Patients – Sexual behavior.
  3. Dementia – Patients – Care. I. Australian Council for Educational
  Research. II. Title
306.70846

FOREWORD

With the growth in numbers of older people over the past several decades there has been considerable focus on ageing, especially in the areas of health, illness, housing and economics. However, little consideration has been given to the emotional needs of our older generation for love, affection and sexual fulfilment. There is a subtle but pervasive attitude in our society that older people have used up their 'humanness'; that they are almost certainly asexual, withered in body and firmly anchored in the past. This picture does not match the facts that are gradually emerging from older people as they are becoming more outspoken on their own behalf. It is becoming clear that old people still need the warmth and caresses of a close companionship and have a capacity for intimacy and sexual pleasure. This is no less so for a person who is affected by dementia where the giving and receiving of affection and intimacy may be the most meaningful link he or she has with others.

People with dementia may have significant difficulties relating to others in their lives, if only because of ubiquitous memory loss and problems with communication. It is important, however, to recognise that people with the commonest type of dementia, Alzheimer's disease, frequently retain their basic personalities, their capacity for love and affection, the ability to express their emotions and their capacity for close relationships well into the course of the disease, because of the sparing of important frontal lobe brain functions in this disorder. It is true that, as a consequence of a dementia illness, some people may develop unpleasant personality traits or lose the characteristics that are necessary to maintain relationships. This is more common in the nursing home setting as the illness progresses and with other dementias which affect the frontal lobe brain functions. There may be a change in a person's sexual activity, sometimes in the form of an increased or decreased demand for sexual gratification, sometimes by expressing sexual desires in ways that are often judged to be indecent or sexually aggressive. Partners particularly, and families, are usually bewildered as to why these changes take place and can be seriously disturbed by them, uncertain how to cope, and may have great difficulty in developing new patterns of relating to the individual. Professional careworkers presented with complex problems of a sexual nature can often find themselves placing these problems low on the list of priorities in a busy schedule. With over 70 per cent of residents in nursing homes and dementia-specific hostels in some stage of dementia, sexual desire and impulsive sexual behaviour are often major concerns, placing extra pressure on staff who are often already stressed by the demands of dementia care.

From her long experience in the field of aged and dementia care, both as a practitioner and a family carer, Barbara Sherman draws on the stories of professionals, home carers and people with dementia to illustrate her points. She frankly confronts the issues of old age, intimacy and sexuality and their implications for service recipients, families and careworkers, often posing contentious issues for thoughtful discussion. She explores the influence that our beliefs and attitudes have on the way we may judge such behaviours. She reminds us that if our aim is to provide a familiar lifestyle for older people who are recipients of our service, then sexuality and the meeting of intimate needs have to be considered as an inclusive part of that lifestyle. This message has implications for the policy formulation of service providers, especially those who offer residential services and a responsibility for a clear explanation of policy to potential residents and/or their representatives. Educators, too, will see the necessity of fostering in careworkers an understanding of the needs for intimate affection and the ways in which these can be appropriately met as well as facilitating their knowledge of the nature of the sexual behaviour of the person with dementia. This book is a welcome addition to the literature on the care of aged persons with its focus on emotions, intimacy and sexuality and on the positive aspects of 'behaviour' in older people needing services and dementia care.

Professor G.A. (Tony) Broe
Professor of Geriatric Medicine
Director of the Centre for Education and Research on Ageing
University of Sydney/Concord Hospital

ACKNOWLEDGEMENTS

I would like to thank all those family carers who have entrusted me to present their stories as sensitively as I know how. My thanks too, to all the participants who took part in my workshops and seminars on sexuality, intimacy and dementia and whose ideas have enriched this book. I have valued my discussions with Jill Pretty, previously Director of Nursing, McQuoin Park, Waitara, NSW, Pam Kerr of Chandos Nursing Home at Ashfield, NSW, Sharon Kratiuk-Wall and Dr Laura Ahmed of the Centre on Education and Research on Ageing, University of Sydney/Concord Hospital, NSW; thanks to Deborah Friend of the Office of the Public Guardian and Tasha Olsen of the Ageing and Disability Department, NSW, Jenny Hill, librarian at the Alzheimers Association, NSW for supplying me with material and information and to Jo Watson of Health Education Services, Ballarat, for feedback from workshops conducted in Ballarat, Victoria. I have particularly valued my contact with Dr Mike Bird, research fellow at the Australian National University who, over the past few years, has given up his time to discuss various issues with me as well as sharing his very valuable research into behaviours associated with dementia. I am also indebted to him for his critical evaluation of the finished manuscript and for supplying me with detailed feedback from seminars in which I participated in 1996 and 1997 in Canberra, ACT and Hornsby, NSW. I also appreciate the permission of the Australian Association of Social Workers to reproduce the Social Workers' Code of Ethics and to Karen Byatt of the Department of Ageing and Disability, NSW for permission to reprint the section on Rights and Responsibilities of Workers from the *Legal Issues Manual* produced by the Department. To my friend and colleague, Ursula Kolbe, my appreciation for her continuing support and for the contribution of her significant artistic skills to the sensitive representations of intimacy. I would like to conclude my thanks by acknowledging those people who wish to remain anonymous who read, corrected and contributed their invaluable expertise.

CONTENTS

ABOUT THIS BOOK

Sex, Intimacy and Aged Care is about the often taboo subject of the sexuality of people who are sixty-five years of age and more. It has been written to promote a greater understanding of the sexuality of old people, in particular those with dementia, and of behaviour that is perceived to be of a sexual nature. It is also written for families who have an older member who is resident in a nursing home or hostel or who are caring at home for a relative who is affected by dementia.

Old people still have longings for love and affection and, for many, the need for sexual gratification remains. These needs are generally unrecognised especially in residential care. In nursing homes and special hostels old people, particularly those with dementia, often go 'hugless'. They are treated as though they are asexual and their needs for intimate relationships are ignored.

In order to throw some light on the way that our learning about sex influences our values about sexual behaviour, I have referred to a growing-up experience that is typical of many people in Australia who are now over seventy years of age. I have also suggested how different social, religious and generational attitudes impact on the understanding and care of old people generally.

During the past two years I have spoken and listened to some 2000 professional carers and family caregivers in seminars and workshops throughout Australia on the topic of sexuality and intimacy in aged care, focusing on those with dementia. As much as possible I have addressed their concerns, represented their opinions and incorporated their suggestions in this book.

It is estimated that over 60 per cent of all residents in nursing homes have some form of dementia. Added to this number are those who are accommodated in dementia-specific hostels. As well, more than half of all people diagnosed with dementia are being cared for in their own homes. Of all the behaviours that people with dementia develop, that which is sexual or is interpreted as sexual can be the most problematic to confront. Sexual behaviour that is uncharacteristic, or which is considered indecent, can be a heartbreaking experience for the families and friends of those affected with dementia. Spouses and partners are often at a loss to understand these changes and do not know how to respond to them. They may not know where to turn to seek help and may be too embarrassed to discuss intimate relationships with either friends or professionals.

Service providers who work in the home can be unsure how to respond when old people behave in a way that seems to be sexual or sensual, often uncertain how to communicate a caring attitude in case someone of the opposite sex 'gets the wrong message'. In residential care people who are cut off from the warmth of intimate relationships that they previously enjoyed in their own homes may reach out to staff and other residents for affection. Where a number of people of both genders live in close proximity to each other and with staff, there are opportunities for relationships that may be, or may appear to be, sexual. Behaviour that is considered to be sexually immoral or indecent or otherwise unacceptable can create complex situations for careworkers to deal with and it is not uncommon for problems to become compounded, particularly when residents, staff and families hold disparate values about sex and sensuality. Such circumstances require sensitive handling in order to avoid misunderstanding or even conflict.

Careworkers will recognise many of the dilemmas outlined in this book and may find that the methods and techniques I have suggested will assist in resolving some of the problem situations they encounter. The anecdotal experiences of others included may go some way towards easing the pain for those families who are or have been troubled by changes in sexual behaviour associated with dementia.

The personal stories may help carers realise that others have the same experiences as they do, and so will feel freer to engage in more open discussion about sexuality. I hope that what I have written will promote discussion and a greater understanding of the sexual needs of older people, the nature of sexual intimacy in old age and, in particular, the sensuality and sexual behaviour of people affected by dementia.

To preserve confidentiality, names and minor details have been changed in the stories used throughout the book.

Barbara Sherman
Sydney, Australia 1998

HOW TO USE THIS BOOK

There are many ways you can use this book.

If you are a service provider you may wish to learn more about sexuality and old people, but might not have the time because of pressure of work to sit down and read a whole book. Use *Sex, Intimacy and Aged Care* as a reference book. Just look up the index for the topic you are interested in, for example, 'sexual abuse' or 'duty of care' and you will find the different sections of the book where these topics are mentioned. However, I recommend that you read the first two sections of the book carefully. The exercises in section 4 are designed so that you can selectively use them to further your knowledge.

If you are a student undertaking a course in gerontological nursing or one with a component on aged care, you will need to read the whole book. One of the main aims of the book is to promote discussion and some of the contentious issues explored in the various sections should provide sufficient material for lively debate.

You might be a caregiver or someone who is interested in the subject of sexuality and old age. Take your time to browse leisurely through the book. Discuss some of the issues next time you are at your support group meeting. Bring this often taboo subject out into the open in a conversation with friends.

Educators should find both the content and the exercises useful when introducing the topic of aged care.

Enjoy your reading.

SECTION

1

Sexuality

and

old age

CHAPTER 1

Thoughts and myths

What is meant by sex and sensuality?

When most people talk about sex and sensuality they are referring to the act of intercourse or genital sex and the physical pleasure that is experienced from this activity. In some cases they will extend the meaning to include sexual play. This is, of course, a very narrow definition of what makes up a person's sexuality and an even narrower definition when we consider all the factors that go to make up an intimate relationship between two people.

Sex and sensuality encompass a kaleidoscope of feelings and activities; from the deepest longings for mutual affection to the simple enjoyment of the company of a loved one. Sexuality also covers a gamut of behaviours — touching, kissing, caressing and cuddling, genital intercourse with mutual orgasm and feelings of closeness and of being wanted and valued as a human being.

Some thoughts on sexuality

In most cultures sex and sexuality are surrounded by strong emotions. Practices, beliefs and taboos about sex have been passed down from generation to generation and have shaped the values that have become part of different religious and cultural heritages. Attitudes about sexual intimacy and sexual morality are deeply entrenched in most of us and are often inflexible and resistant to change, probably more so than other values we hold.

We are also subject to a whole host of sexual myths which, together with our culturally and religiously determined beliefs, condition the values we hold about sex generally. When it comes to old people, what we believe about their sexual needs and practices colours our ideas and will often prejudice the way we judge the behaviour of people in this age group.

In fact, sex and old age are not very often discussed in the same breath at all. If the subject does come up, we tend to skirt around it by using more delicate language such as the word intimacy rather than sex or sexual intercourse. Seldom do we hear words like passion, desire and making love used in connection with older people. Many books about ageing and articles in professional journals tend to ignore sexuality altogether. It doesn't exist! Or the subject is dismissed in a line or two. Yet sexuality and making love are part of the fabric of our lives; part of the very essence of being human – even for older people.

One of the most commonly held beliefs about old people who exhibit or admit to sexual desire is that they are a bit weird, perverted, or at the very least not quite normal. The young man who has led a sexually active life and acts out his desire in old age is often criticised as being lecherous or licentious. Society can be even more judgemental about the woman of sixty or more who enjoys a sexual life. She is often labelled 'nymphomaniac' or 'oversexed' or it is said that 'at her age she should know better'. When we hear of a couple in their seventies or eighties marrying, we may react with either disapproval or faint patronage and refer to them as being 'cute' or 'sweet'. Or we may think it is a bit of a joke. Some people have difficulty in accepting that their parents have a sex life, even though the fact that they themselves exist puts paid to that doubt. But someone their grandmother's age? Well, that doesn't bear thinking about!

Of course it is a fact that some older people do not have, or do not want, a sexual life. Some couples find that after years of marriage they have become bored with sex and are satisfied with companionship centred on non-sexual activities. Sadly, other marriages have deteriorated to a point where even the satisfaction of a warm companionship has long since disappeared. Old people who have lost their partners may feel that it is disloyal to the dead partner to have a sexual liaison with somebody else. Others might actively search for a 'soulmate'. Many women, in particular, are deprived of a sexual relationship after losing a life partner even though the need for gratification may still be strong. There are people who have experienced sexual difficulties for many years and, not seeking help, carry these difficulties into older age. In some situations, ill health, incontinence or physical disability are barriers to a full and satisfying sex life, although medical attention can often overcome these problems.

Myths about sex and old age

A whole host of myths has grown up around the sexual behaviour of older people. Here are some of the more common ones.

Myth: Old people can't or don't do it

This is one of the most pervasive myths — that older people are not able to indulge in sexual activity. Or don't want to. They have lost the urge or they are not physically able. They are past it! If they do have sex, they shouldn't. Somehow it's wrong, even indecent. Either way, when this myth is believed, it is a no-win situation for older couples.

Older love is gentler than young love. In older age the gymnastics of the twenty- or thirty-year-old will undoubtedly have given way to much smoother techniques of love-making. There is invariably more emphasis on caressing and cuddling and sexual play, rather than the hasty and spontaneous acts of a younger age group. Sometimes older people do not wish to engage in actual intercourse as often as before. A woman's sexual interest may decrease with age or an erection may be a little more difficult for the man to obtain, or the sensation at ejaculation different from when he was younger. However, it is not true that a woman's sexual life is finished after menopause. Some women say that the first time they experienced an orgasm was after they had gone through the change of life. These women often confide that fear of falling pregnant in the days before the pill – when contraceptive techniques were clumsy and not always safe – caused them to 'have a headache' or pretend to be asleep. After menopause they are able to enjoy love-making without the anxiety of unwanted pregnancy.

Women in their eighties report experiencing orgasm, as have men of that age. For many the passion burns as brightly as it always has. Many a couple who has formed a new liaison in the latter part of life will express amazement at the depth of the sexual feeling for the new partner and the excitement that the relationship kindled.

A reported low incidence of sexual activity among older people in studies conducted earlier this century is now thought to be incorrect because of the tendency not to include this age group in the populations surveyed. Dr Alex Comfort (1976) points out that as far as a sex life was concerned, older people were not included 'because everybody knew that they had none and they were assumed to have none, because nobody asked'.

More recent studies conducted exclusively on this age group are considered to give a much truer picture than earlier projects such as the Kinsey report (1948) and others. For instance, a study carried out with people living in retirement villages (see Woolford, 1996), found that 63 per cent of male residents and 30 per cent of females between the ages of eighty and 102 years of age occasionally engaged in sexual intercourse. One study conducted by a research team from Duke University (Pfeiffer et al, 1968) in the United States surveyed 254 people of both sexes over a five-year period. They found that the median age for ceasing to have sexual intercourse in this group was sixty-eight years. The age when men stopped sexual activity ranged between forty-nine and ninety years. For women it was between sixty and eight-one years and a reason given for the lesser upper age limit of women was because of the lack of partners, not lack of interest. Over the five-year period 16 per cent of those who were followed up reported that there was a fall-off in sexual intercourse, while 14 per cent said that their sexual activity had increased.

In studying the sexual activity of married couples over sixty years of age, it was found that the following age groups engaged in intercourse at least once a month:

Age	
60–65	65%
66–70	55%
71–75	45%
76+	24%

Myth: Old people don't enjoy sex

We age the way we live. People tend to have the same desires and behave in much the same way as they grow older. The person who did not enjoy a satisfying sex life when she or he was younger, may not be interested in old age. However, when people have always experienced an active sex life, the chances are that they will continue to feel much the same way when they are older. Fifty-four per cent of men and women between the ages of sixty and ninety-three years studied by Newman and Nicholls (1960) reported that they had not experienced any significant decrease in sexual activity between sixty and seventy-five years. One quarter of them over seventy-five years was sexually active and any decline experienced was exclusively because of ill health or ill health of a partner.

The enjoyment experienced from making love lasts for many people into their seventies and eighties and even into their nineties. It is not unusual for couples to say that their sex life is much more satisfying for them as they get older, partly because the financial anxiety and other worries of supporting a home and rearing a family and 'getting on in life', are no longer creating pressure in their lives. They say they feel free to devote more time and thought to each other. For many, love-making has developed a richness born of years of experience with the sexual mistakes of youth satisfactorily resolved.

Romance still adds colour and delight to the lives of many older people. The following poem entitled 'For Us' encapsulates the feelings that many older people have about sexual intimacy.

> Sex after sixty, a delightful pleasure
> To be sipped, enjoyed and savoured at leisure
> No tearing away at undershorts, zippers,
> No frantic fumbling of hooks and grippers.
> Time to explore those still unknown –
> Each and every erogenous zone.
> No fretful, teething baby's cry
> To interrupt a lover's sigh,
> Just the warmth of each other's embrace,
> Fingers tracing a familiar face.
> No more worry about periods due.
> We've indulged before, but forever it's new,
> And when we total up the accounts,
> It's quality, not quantity, that counts.
>
> *Friedlander*

Myth: Old people aren't sexually attractive

One of our twentieth century fantasies is that only the young and the beautiful are sexually attractive. Films and television, magazines and billboards all reinforce this stereotype. How often do you see an advertisement featuring older people that has a sexual flavour? Rather, publicity that is aimed at older people, even those in their fifties, gives us a benign image of some companionable activity – gardening with the grandchildren, preparing a barbecue for the family, bushwalking. If they are aimed at older people still, we see a group doing gentle exercises in a swimming pool or a woman sitting in a recliner chair surrounded by generations of family. Old age is often presented in the media with the image of a person hobbling along on a walking stick or some apathetic old person being pushed along in a wheelchair — often regardless of the news item it is meant to portray. These are 'ageist' images about old people that are commonly held by people who are not yet old.

Sexual attraction does not necessarily diminish as people get older. Many old people say that they are more in love with their partner than ever before. Part of this love is sexual attraction. In his autobiography published in 1985 when he was in his ninetieth year, the famous artist Lloyd Rees wrote:

> In certain ways, we are closer now, after fifty-three years of marriage, for there's a human closeness between us that's very beautiful ... It was not till I was first married at over thirty years of age that I knew sexual expression, but this is not to deny its tremendous influence on my life. It gave colour and warmth to almost everything and a heightened appreciation of the arts, and one should not imagine for a moment that it necessarily decreases with the years, for it certainly hasn't in my case. I am all in sympathy with the French writer, Colette, who when asked in a press interview, 'And do you regret the passing of the emotions of love?' replied, 'Fancy asking me such a question — I'm only seventy-five!'

When people who are now in their seventies and older were young, sexual attraction was sometimes called 'It'. 'It' was more than just physical beauty. It was personal magnetism, it was pleasantness, interest, enthusiasm for life, and all the positive traits that draw people to one another. The French actress Mistinguett was renowned for her charisma and sexual magnetism in her eighties, and Hermoine Gingold took a lover when she was eighty-one. History is full of such anecdotes. One of the most famous 'sex symbols' of this century was Mae West, the 'Come up and see me sometime' actress, whose sexuality was still apparent in great old age. We can probably all think of an old person in our lives who fulfils the role of a sexy oldie.

CHAPTER
2

Beliefs, values and attitudes

Since most of us can remember, we have been taught the morality of our particular culture or sub-culture by our parents, school and the mentors of our particular religion. Over the centuries sexual practices, rituals, sanctions and taboos have become part of the fabric of our different religious and cultural heritages; part of the cement of our various modern-day societies. And each religion and culture presents its beliefs, attitudes and customs as the right ones. However, our attitudes are often based on ignorance and superstition rather than logic. It is said that, while the origin of many of the beliefs and values about things sexual has long since been lost in time, the emotions that were originally associated with them have remained. For instance, many people believe that Adam and Eve when committing the original sin, became so ashamed of their bodies that they covered their nakedness. Shame associated with nakedness still persists, yet common sense would have to ask why this first couple should be ashamed of the bodies that God had given them.

Generational values

Taboos and morality about things sexual do modify somewhat from generation to generation and we embrace the general sexual values and customs of our particular culture in the time in which we live. We tend to hold on to these values throughout our lives.

Values within the family

While members of one family generally share the same basic cultural and religious values about morality and sexual behaviour there are often marked generational differences within the family. When children are young, they tend to accept the sexual behaviour of their parents without question. But by the time they have developed their own sexuality and sexual practices, adult children may find it hard to accept that the lives of their parents have a sexual component. When this is the case adult children can become severely embarrassed when elderly parents enter into a sexual relationship with a new partner. In some cases they actively discourage it and may put intolerable pressure on the old couple to separate in order to avoid family disagreement.

Maureen was convinced that her father had 'lost his mind' or had been unduly influenced by a woman resident in the hostel where they lived, when he announced that he was taking her for a trip overseas. However, her sister and brother approved, encouraging the couple in their plans for a more permanent relationship. Maureen applied considerable pressure to prevent the couple from achieving their plans, ranging from asking the hostel administration to take action, directing the travel agent to cancel the tickets and seeking legal advice as to how she could prevent the relationship. All to no avail. She even tried to convince people that her father had dementia. Eventually her father married his lady but as time went on the rift between her father, sister and brother — who approved of the relationship — and Maureen worsened.

In this sort of family situation, money or a perceived threat to the family member's inheritance can sometimes be an issue. This was not the case here.

Values and residential care

There can be as many as three generations in a staff of any one nursing home or hostel, each generation with different values, beliefs and attitudes about sexual behaviour. Even within the same age group there can be a wide variety of learning and experience and each one will invariably be convinced that she or he knows best when it comes to dealing with the sexual conduct of residents. The resident and resident's family may also have different generational attitudes as well as cultural and religious beliefs. So, within one facility, there are often many different and at times conflicting views. These differences must be handled sensitively in order to prevent misunderstanding. When a situation of conflicting attitudes arises, dialogue among every one involved should be encouraged in an attempt to resolve the differences.

Our emotions also play a very large part in influencing the way we regard sexuality and intimacy, particularly when dealing with dependent old people. At a workshop conducted by the Australian Capital Territory Dementia Care Network in 1996, dementia care staff identified the following emotions that they considered significant in connection with their work:

- empathy, sadness
- personal vulnerability:
  - identification – 'this could happen to me when I get old'
  - fear/anxiety in threatening situations such as physical resistance or harassment in the shower
- embarrassment
- strong desire to suppress emotions, such as:
  - personal discomfort with sexual matters
  - dislike of resident's family or of a resident
- devastation at resident's distress.

Cultural and religious values

Attitudes about sensuality and sexual behaviour vary from culture to culture and from religion to religion. What may be considered abnormal or immoral in one culture, may be quite usual and acceptable behaviour in another. For instance, many cultures believe that sex before marriage is sinful. Others actively encourage sexual experience, particularly for young men, believing that a man owes it to his wife to have had some sexual experience. Exposure of any part of a woman's body is considered to be sexually immoral in some cultures, while in others it is not even remarkable. In some societies frequent kissing between males is considered to be normal behaviour, but in others this sort of action may be regarded with suspicion. Hugging a person of the opposite gender may be a gross invasion of privacy for some, and even taboo in some ethnic groups.

In a multicultural society such as Australia it is not unusual for staff in nursing homes and hostels to have been brought up in different cultures and sub-cultures with different experiences and sets of moral values which can be at odds with those of the residents and other members of staff. Because of this, behaviour of a resident can be misinterpreted or residents may get a wrong message from the way the worker behaves towards them.

Effects of attitudes

There are times when attitudes about sexual behaviour held by careworkers, and at times families, carry over into other areas of the life of an older person and affect the way they are treated. Since sexuality in older people is seldom perceived in a positive way, there is always a risk that there will be a bias against certain sexual practices. This may have undesirable consequences both for the person whose behaviour it is and the person who is judging the behaviour.

In a dementia-specific hostel one careworker became fond of two residents there. She went to some trouble to arrange for them to visit the local Returned Services Club; made small purchases for them, took them shopping and other outings and generally took a very special interest in them. This came to an abrupt halt when she discovered that they had lived in a long-time lesbian relationship and were not cousins as she had previously thought. She found that she lost all interest in the two old ladies and would avoid helping them to shower and dress unless there was no one else there to carry out the task. The religious belief of this careworker prohibited her from accepting homosexuality in any form. In a very short time she applied for a transfer to another section of the complex. This was a satisfactory outcome for her in the short term, but she recognised that at some later date she may be faced with the same circumstances.

During the past few years, consistent with the recognition of the benefits of providing a more home-like atmosphere for people in residential care, there has been a more enlightened approach to intimacy needs at least in some facilities. Some places now provide shared accommodation for couples; sometimes even for those who, although unmarried, have shared a life together. There is also a growing trend to provide spaces for residents to have privacy for affectionate moments with a visiting partner. Even for making love.

However, there are still nursing homes where staff or administration or both hold strong beliefs that sexual intercourse is only for the purpose of procreation or that a nursing home is not a 'right and proper place' for people to cohabit or even openly display affection. Where this is an institutional view, the policy is often to disallow couples to share rooms or to deny space and opportunity for residents to engage in intimate moments with visiting partners. These restrictions are vindicated for the staff of that facility if an adult son or daughter says, 'Well you know mum and dad don't get on'. But would it not be better to build on whatever it is that has kept mum and dad together for the past fifty or so years? Or better still ask mum and dad what they would like to do?

Dr Juan Hitzig (1994) emphasises how illogical some of our attitudes about sex can be with this joke:

You surely all know the story of the [manager of the nursing home] who calls the doctor to complain 'You will have to do something about that patient in room 215, he masturbates all day long!' The doctor moves towards the room and says: 'I can't see anything. Actually the door is closed.' 'Oh', said the manager, 'but you have to stand on this chair and look through the little window on top of the door'.

Staff agreement

Residential careworkers who are often comparative strangers to the resident, have the power to influence and control the moment-to-moment life of that person. So sexual values that are held by staff of nursing homes and hostels will often determine how sexual behaviour is judged and the way residents and, to a lesser extent, families are treated. Complications can often arise because careworkers cannot agree on what is considered to be appropriate sexual behaviour.

In one nursing home, staff were asked what sexual behaviours of dementia residents they found difficult to cope with. In previous discussion, they were certain that all would agree on the actions of which they would disapprove whereas, when put to the test, they could only reach consensus on just four behaviours they considered to be unacceptable. Behaviour that presented problems for some were thought by others to be tolerable, even though they did not necessarily approve of them. Overall the behaviours that presented problems for them were numerous and covered a wide range. It can be seen from the list on page 17 that:

- attitudes to many of these behaviours have a general moral bias rather than a sexual flavour
- some of the behaviours would be expected and acceptable in a person's own home
- some of the behaviours would usually be associated with friendship rather than sexuality.

This highlights a major difficulty for service providers, especially those whose work is in residential care facilities and respite services. How do we define and judge a dementia resident's 'sexual' behaviour? Is it a moral issue? Do we have the same attitudes towards pilfering and 'story-telling' which are also common behavioural characteristics of dementia? Do we make assumptions when we interpret behaviour as sexual? For example, do we believe

'Sexual' behaviours that staff found difficult to cope with*

- Married couples sharing a room/showering together
- Any two residents of the opposite sex continually seeking each other's company
- Residents of the opposite sex spending much of their time together, if one or both were married
- Residents of the opposite sex holding hands
- Stroking, cuddling, hugging, kissing
- Visiting each other's rooms, particularly if door closed, and lying on bed
- Gay and lesbian relationships
- Intimacy with visiting spouse or partner
- Intercourse with visiting spouse or partner
- Resident and partner sharing the shower
- Lewd language
- Suggestive actions and words towards staff or other residents
- Masturbating
- Undressing and public exposure (male and female)
- Harassment — touching, fondling, sexual approach

* Behaviours named as sexual and difficult by thirty-two staff from a dementia facility with a predominantly mobile resident population.

that it is 'wrong' for residents to form a hand-holding relationship when both have a living spouse or do we consider that they might have found a way to fulfil their needs for affection? These are just some of the questions we need to ask ourselves, before we react.

While we may not wish to significantly change our values about sexuality and morality, to work effectively with older people we must at least try to understand their beliefs, values, desires and inhibitions, and what lies behind their behaviour. We must also become aware and question our own values, attitudes and prejudices and recognise how they impact on each other and the lives of those in our care. Developing some insight into our own sexuality too, goes a long way towards helping us understand the sexuality of others.

3

Values and attitudes of older people

If we ever do discuss the sexuality of older people, we give little or no consideration to their beliefs and attitudes about sex. Sexual practices have not greatly altered over the years; what has happened over the last decade or so in some cultures is a greater permissiveness in sexual behaviour and the freedom to talk about things sexual. This has, to a large extent, lifted the burden of embarrassment and guilt that once accompanied reference to anything that even bordered on the topic of sexuality.

However, to better appreciate how older people perceive sexuality, it is necessary to not only know what their values are but also to know what experiences have influenced and shaped these attitudes. This understanding is even more important when caring for a person with dementia who is unable to control behaviour or even comprehend or articulate what lies behind her or his sexual actions.

Sexual attitudes

Taboos, inhibitions and censure associated with sensuality and sexual relationships have persisted in some cultures and religions for thousands of years, with little or no change taking place. In other societies and sub-cultures there is an ebb and flow over time which leads to modification of some attitudes, even though the fundamental morals of that society may alter little. For instance, the advent of AIDS led some people to a more enlightened view of homosexual relationships and to a greater emphasis generally on the need for 'safety' among sexually active people.

While there is a wide variation in cultural experience throughout the world, in many countries that follow the Judaeo–Christian ethic attitudes about sexual morality have followed a similar pattern. Consider, for example, a typical growing-up experience that determined the sexual morality of Australians of European descent brought up in Australia approximately three or four generations ago.

Secrecy and ignorance

The majority of people who are now seventy and over were then in a sexual union or becoming aware of the pull of their sexuality. If one factor stands out more than any other for this generation it is the ignorance, secrecy, modesty and suspicion that shrouded anything and everything that was even remotely associated with sex and sensuality. There was no access to sex education as such and while biology classes taught about circulation and digestion, there was generally avoidance of information about the reproductive system, let alone any admission that sexual longings and behaviour existed. The word 'sex' was only used to denote gender. Even on occasions when legitimate pregnancy was talked about it was referred to as 'an interesting condition' or 'in the family way'.

As a general rule parents did not speak to their children about things sexual, possibly because they themselves were ignorant of anything outside of coitus in the missionary position. Many were not aware, until they consulted a doctor, that babies appeared nine months from the date of conception. After all they themselves had been reared by mothers who had been taught that it was indecent even to show their swollen pregnant bodies in public. Nor did parents or the community expect the topics of sex or reproduction to be discussed by school teachers or the school nurse. Country youngsters were invariably more enlightened, living as they did in close proximity to animals and therefore intimately aware of copulation, birth and death. Female cats and dogs were purposefully kept by some city families for the sole intention of providing their children with a 'sex education', though it was unlikely that children got the message that intercourse led to the appearance of the squirming puppy or kitten or that a connection was made between the animal and human. It was equally unlikely that many parents would encourage discussion on the subject. A common reply to searching enquiry was, 'Wait till you're older and then you will understand' or 'When you are older you will know!' And because 'older' seemed a long way off, young people sought other means of enlightenment.

Sexual learning, or more correctly mislearning, mainly took place in the school yard among groups of giggling schoolgirls under the trees or in the shelter sheds at recess and lunch breaks. Boys were equally misinformed and anxious about their own developing bodies and incipient stirrings, and bewildered about the mystery of sexual attraction.

Menstruation for many girls was a time of extreme anxiety. Totally ignorant of the nature of their maturing bodies, some would hide the 'shameful' fact from their parents, self-blaming for some unknown transgression. Parents' warning of 'Mind you don't do anything wrong' was a worry, so that what frequently followed the first kiss were sleepless nights in fear that the inevitable outcome of this indiscretion would be 'having a baby'.

A German acquaintance, discussing her own slim exposure to sex education as a child in the 1930s, remembers only that her mother cautioned, 'Don't ever go to bed with a man' and 'Don't ever sleep with a man'. She says that it was years before she found out that going to bed and sleeping didn't really have anything to do with it! And it was this somewhat coy and pervasive attitude that in years to come burdened many couples with feelings of guilt around sexual intercourse. Even in marriage.

Modesty

This era was an age of temperance and modesty. And modesty was more often than not linked with sexual morality. Except for the very few, conformity to respectability rather than fashion dictated modes of dress. Heavyweight three piece double-breasted suits and shirts with collars suitably starched were the uniform to be worn by men on most occasions. The woman who wore her skirt shorter than mid calf was considered to be 'fast' or 'shameless' and gloves and hats were obligatory, even for shopping expeditions. Threaded through the insistence on covering the female body was the implicit understanding that exposure, of knees even, was an open invitation for all men to 'take advantage'. Equally decorous clothing was worn for sport: cream trousers and long-sleeved shirts for tennis and cricket by males and bloomers that reached almost to the knee by females.

Segregated swimming was still a recent memory for many young people – men and women swimming at different times or in separate locations. Neck-to-knee bathing costumes of the previous era had given way to the more daring heavy woollen numbers, often two-toned, with belts that separated the high-backed top from the bottom that modestly covered the thighs. So deeply entrenched was the custom of modest dressing that when an English fashion model who was an official guest of the Victoria Racing Club turned up at Flemington on Melbourne Cup Day in a mini-skirt in the 1960s it caused a furore. The newspapers of the day were full of condemnatory comments from the nation's leading matrons. The age of casualness and freedom in dress was still half a generation away.

Nakedness was indelicate, even indecent. Full length mirrors were only for checking that a petticoat did not hang below a skirt or so that crooked back seams on silk stockings could be observed and straightened. Some even say that diagnosis of breast cancer was often too late because women were too embarrassed to examine their bodies. With this strong sense of modesty entrenched in youth, many women and men would never dress or undress in front of each other, even when they were married. Before going to bed at night they – and women particularly – would undress in the dark or behind a closed door.

It is understandable then that old people who are now in the position of requiring intimate care either in nursing homes or from visiting professionals in their own homes, are embarrassed and sometimes distressed. Modesty is often the reason that an old person is reluctant to submit to being undressed and bathed by care-workers, a behaviour that is often referred to as 'non-compliant' (see page 24).

Influence of the church

Transport was not so readily available. Young people had very little or no money to spend on fares or entertainment. Very few families owned motor cars, and a young person who could drive was a rarity and usually a member of a rich family. Generally the home was the hub of entertainment and leisure activities and sporting facilities were provided by clubs, usually in the locality. Saturday afternoon at the local cinema was a treat whenever it could be afforded.

In many urban communities, social life and fun for most young people was centred in the church, and the teachings of the various religions had a far greater influence on life than they do today. There was a pervasive emphasis on virtue. Many religions frowned on such frivolities as dancing, make-up and stockingless legs, not to mention any sort of one-to-one relationship between teenage boys and girls. Young people disappearing for a furtive kiss behind the Sunday School building or the school toilet block immediately came under suspicion and, after 'a good talking to', would be under constant surveillance. There was a general acceptance of the rules of proper conduct throughout most of the community, much more so than now. There was a strong ethic in many families that boys were honour bound to 'respect' girls. While it was not openly discussed (and not always observed) young people

Non-compliance

Non-compliance is a term often used by careworkers to describe the behaviour of old people.

What non-compliance seems to mean is that an old person, for reasons we do not understand and which they themselves may not understand, is reluctant or refuses to do something we ask them to do when we want them to do it or will not comply with what we think is best for them. They are disobedient!

Of course the decision as to whether or not we should insist on the person we are caring for complying with our requests or directions is not always easy. Often it is a difficult balancing act between choice and compliance, resistance and insistence or finding the balance between pressure of work and enough time to fully assess and satisfactorily handle a situation. Is it essential that the person does this right now? It might not be of great importance if someone misses out on a shower today although if they are soiled or their face and hands are food-stained, we would consider it our duty to clean the person no matter what. If a person with dementia is walking outside naked we would not hesitate to insist that they be covered against the cold, regardless of their refusal. The same would apply to cases where the person is in a life-threatening situation or, except in certain circumstances, refusing to take essential medication.

Each situation of 'non-compliance' is unique. Before labelling people as non-compliant, assess the reasons for the person's resistance. Many an instance of non-compliance is contributed to by our failure to understand the reasons behind the person's feelings, to respect their wishes and offer choices. If by our actions we let people we care for know that we understand, there is more likelihood that they will cooperate. In considering their stance, we add to their dignity and self-esteem and this must always be of a high priority.

understood that sex before marriage was a definite taboo. Condoms were difficult to find, even if the young man had the money and could pluck up enough courage to make the purchase. There was no contraceptive pill and even married women were often too embarrassed to ask for the contraceptive devices available.

Heavy petting took place in the greatest secrecy accompanied by a good deal of deception and guilt. The consequence of unguarded intercourse was invariably pregnancy with the majority of families unable to cope with the 'shame' of illegitimacy. Many girls were cast out from their families, at least until after the baby was born, and parents and professionals alike exerted influence on the mother to have the baby adopted. Alternatively the pregnant girl might be forced into a backyard abortion with the risk of infection or worse. The common belief was 'Good girls don't have babies' and even when families took a more sympathetic attitude, the young woman herself and often the young man carried a burden of shame and sadness for many years. No counselling then. Not all families were so judgemental. In some large families it was the custom to accept the child as part of the nuclear family, so that many a youngest child was the offspring of an older sister.

Whether it was because of later sexual maturity, a fear of pregnancy or a strong sense of morality, sex before marriage did not seem to be quite as usual as it is today and the first sexual experience often did not happen until young people were in their late teens or twenties. On the rare occasion of a schoolgirl pregnancy, the girl and even her family would be ostracised. In some communities the family had to move away because of the shame.

It was not usual to have a sexual relationship without some sort of commitment although the Second World War saw a modification in this pattern. Young men and women in the armed services were cut adrift from family influence and strict moral boundaries. With the men likely to be sent away to fight and the ever present threat of invasion in Australia, young people lived daily with only a fragile hold on life. Many abandoned the accepted moral code and became involved in short-term sexual relationships. Young wives left at home alone for years while their husbands were away at war turned elsewhere for support.

It is not hard to understand and appreciate that this mixture of virtue, ignorance, misinformation, secrecy, suspicion, shame and fear has placed some of today's older people in conflict about their own sexuality and that of others. It is no wonder that many are reluctant to talk openly about sex and are embarrassed or ignore it altogether when the subject comes up. What is remarkable, is that there are older people with this growing-up experience who are open-minded about things sexual. They often appear more tolerant of the sexual behaviour of others, than some younger people. One explanation is that the open discussion and change of community attitudes about sex over the past few decades has given older people 'permission' to feel freer to accept their own sexuality. Now it is up to a younger generation to also recognise and understand the sexuality of old people.

Sexuality

and

dementia

4

The effect of dementia on sexual behaviour

Dementia is a disorder of thinking and behaviour that occurs as a result of changes that take place in the brain. It is caused by diseases that progressively attack and damage the cells that make up the mass of brain tissue. The most common of these conditions is dementia of the Alzheimer's type which accounts for about 60 per cent of all cases diagnosed, followed by multi-infarct or vascular dementia, comprising approximately 17 per cent of cases. There are many other dementia conditions that are less common. Dementia, particularly of the Alzheimer's type, is progressive, it worsens over time and as yet there is no known cure, treatment or way of preventing it or significantly slowing its progression.

The person who is affected by dementia becomes progressively handicapped and finds it increasingly difficult to cope with the demands of everyday life. Behaviour, including sexual behaviour, undergoes significant changes and there is usually a marked alteration in the person's demeanour or personality. Not everyone is affected in the same way; patterns of disability and retained abilities and behaviour vary from person to person.

Cognitive changes in dementia

Characteristically people with dementia experience a loss of memory as well as disturbances of thinking and judgement and the capacity to formulate logical and realistic ideas. Concentration will be impaired and over time there will be a decline in comprehension of what is going on around them and what is being said to them. Failure to recognise people, even those closest to them, is common as is the inability to identify objects and their use. These disabilities are called **cognitive** defects and the main characteristic of dementia is always cognitive impairment. The confusion that results from these disabilities makes the world a difficult and often frightening place to live in. Depending on the seriousness of cognitive defects, the person will become dependent on others for care to a greater or lesser extent.

Affective changes in dementia

As well as cognitive changes, there are usually changes in the person's emotional make-up and mood to the point where the personality is markedly altered. This is called a change in affect. The consequences of dementia may render someone anxious and fearful. Another person may develop personality traits opposite to those displayed before the dementia; a hitherto gentle and easygoing person may become irritable and aggressive or agitated, restless and overactive. A person previously active and assertive may become withdrawn and listless. Normal traits can become exaggerated; the 'private' person becomes more isolated, withdrawn and listless while the assertive person exhibits aggressive and, on rare occasions, violent behaviour.

It is important to note that while aggression, listlessness and loss of initiative are often associated with changes taking place in the brain, there is also a possibility that these traits may be a reaction to something in the person's environment such as frustration, misunderstanding, provocation or boredom. Such factors should always be considered as triggers for alteration in mood or emotional affect. Depression associated with dementia is not uncommon. There are people whose dementia causes them to be melancholy, listless and uninterested and depression should always be considered as the underlying reason for this behaviour.

If we add suspiciousness often to the point of paranoia, delusions and hallucinations to the above characteristics, we have a mix of personality traits and cognitive defects that results in serious confusion. This makes the world a difficult, even frightening place for the person with dementia to live in, and creates significant problems in the initiating and maintaining of relationships with others.

Changes in sexual behaviour

As with other behaviour, changes in sexual behaviour are frequent in people affected by dementia. The results of one study (Derouesné et al, 1996) suggest that 87 per cent of people with dementia of the Alzheimer's type experience a decrease in sexual activity, while in 13 per cent there is an increase. In this same study a minority of the people surveyed exhibited a decreased sense of decency or did 'embarrassing things'.

Increased demand

When a person with dementia exhibits a marked increase in the demand for sexual gratification, she or he is often labelled 'oversexed'. However, great care should be taken in attaching such labels as oversexed or lecherous to anyone. Consider the reasons that might be contributing to the behaviour:

- damage to the cerebral cortex could be the reason for sexual hunger
- prescription drugs could be increasing sexual drive
- external stimuli could be inciting sexual impulse
- possibilities for pleasure may be now so limited that physical gratification is all that the person has left.

Consider also that the sexual needs of the dementing person may always have been at a high level, a 'normal' need that has carried over to the present time. Alternatively, the person who shows little or no interest in sex, may have always had a relatively limited sexual appetite.

Patterns in sexual behaviour

Service providers and families alike report that changes in sexual behaviour are associated with other behavioural changes that take place. They observe that the person whose affective behaviour has changed – in particular someone who has become withdrawn and apathetic and has generally lost interest in life – will most probably experience a marked decline in sexual interest. Conversely an increase in the person's libido or heightened activity in seeking sexual gratification tends to be associated with restlessness and irritability. A study carried out by Derouesné et al. from the Department of Neurology, Hôpital de la Salpetriere, Paris, France in 1995, on people with dementia of the Alzheimer's type tends to confirm these personal observations. They found that changes in sexual behaviour did not correlate with the cognitive defects of dementia or the severity of the disease. Rather the changes were associated with affective disabilities or mood disorders, as well as the general level of the person's activity. Age did not appear to be a significant factor in changes in sexual behaviour.

There do seem to be exceptions to these findings. From time to time a partner or careworker will insist that a person whose general behaviour is characterised by vagueness, gentleness and apathy will show an increased demand for sexual gratification. Each person has his or her individual reactions to a dementing illness.

Gender differences

There is no apparent difference in the occurrence of changes in sexual behaviour between men and women although some suggest that the type of behaviour differs. It is a general impression that men are invariably more sexually aggressive than women, and this aggression is often associated with sexual harassment or lewd language. While these behaviours do seem to be more common, or more noticeable, in men rather than in women, women are also known to display these traits. Women are sometimes reported to be assertive, even aggressive in their demands for sexual gratification while some men appear to be indifferent to sexual activity.

An early sign of dementia

Sometimes a change in sexual behaviour is one of the early signs of dementia. A spouse or careworker will recall that a change in demand for sex or an aberration in other behaviour of a sexual nature, preceded a diagnosis of dementia.

> John and Judy Hunter were in their middle fifties. Like her husband, Judy was a lawyer and worked in a busy suburban practice. Judy's sexual appetite began to increase until she was demanding intercourse several times in one night. When she began to react with extreme irritation to office staff pointing out errors she was making in connection with her briefs, they thought she was experiencing burnout. They suggested that she take a holiday. Some time later Judy was diagnosed with Alzheimer's disease.

Retained sexual values

Because of the strength of sexual beliefs and early training, some dementia-affected people retain their values about sex for a long time, albeit in a somewhat muddled way. As has already been noted, many older people were brought up with the idea that there is something not quite nice about a naked body; that nakedness is associated with sexuality and is a bit shameful. This attitude may persist in older age even with people who have dementia.

> Normally Joseph Cohen was a gentle man but he had become extremely aggressive with the home care aides who came to shower him. It wasn't hard to guess that he was embarrassed at being undressed and showered by strange young women in his own home. He also refused to accept the explanation that young women dressed in T-shirts and jeans were nurses — his memory of a nurse was a woman in a starched white uniform.

Similar situations are common in nursing homes. Imagine how embarrassed someone with a deeply ingrained sense of modesty must feel at being undressed or toiletted by a strange person, in a strange place — particularly if there is no consideration for privacy. Because of this modesty, residents might invent a string of excuses as to why they can't be showered right now, or they might become agitated or determinedly uncooperative. Sometimes residents will try to hang on to urine or faeces rather than have staff of the opposite sex help them to the toilet. Occasionally a person will exhibit behaviour for which there seems to be no logical reason. It may well be that it is a consequence of the resident's sexual values being threatened.

On a consultancy in a dementia unit some time ago, while I was waiting for the manager, staff asked me to see a new resident, an eighty-year-old woman whose behaviour was puzzling them. She had been distressed since early morning and now was packed up ready to leave. When I finally won her confidence she explained to me, very tearfully, that the people there, meaning the staff, wanted her to become engaged to a boy there, but she couldn't do this because soon she was going to be married to another boy. She said they would be angry with her when they found out so she was going to have to leave.

What she said to me was, 'He took off all my clothes and he touched me on my body', but she impressed on me that he really was 'a very nice boy'. What she was referring to, of course, was being helped to shower by a male personal care assistant that morning. The values of this particular woman told her that you only took off your clothes in front of a man if you were married to him or you were going to marry him. Once staff knew what lay behind the behaviour, a female personal careworker was assigned to shower and toilet her. Other steps they took to make her comfortable were:
- telling her beforehand that they were going to the shower or toilet

- explaining that staff were nurses and she needed their care right now
- using large bath towels or a towelling robe to cover her body before and after showering, which cut down on the need for body contact
- encouraging her to wash herself
- gradually introducing male staff into non-intimate activities.

With a reassuring and sensitive approach, male staff were eventually reintroduced into her total care.

Often a family caregiver comes up with an innovative solution to a situation where sexual modesty is creating a problem.

A woman with dementia was being cared for in her own home by her son. She was able to bath and dress herself independently, but one day she called to her son, 'I can't get out of the bath!' 'Don't worry,' he replied, 'I'll come and help you out.' But she refused to let him come into the bathroom, saying that she did not have any clothes on and he would see her, and it wasn't right for a son to see his mother naked. 'How about if you shut your eyes while I help you out,' he said, 'then I won't see you?' So she shut her eyes tight and the situation was saved.

Misinterpreting words and actions

It is not unusual for the words and actions of caregivers to be interpreted by a person with dementia as having a sexual meaning. It is essential to make sure that actions are fully explained and that, as far as possible, what is being said to or asked of a person with dementia is understood.

A resident in a special purpose hostel developed a catastrophic reaction (see page 37), becoming incoherent and distraught. Each time the night nurses came to change her wet bed, they would find her fully dressed and lying on top of the bedclothes so they would change her back into her nightdress. She would ask them, 'Why are you doing this?' and they would reply, 'Because we love you'. She was in terror that the words 'love you' had a sexual meaning. When the nurses understood this they would answer her query by telling her that they were changing her nightdress to make her more comfortable. Her panic reaction disappeared.

It is characteristic for a dementing person to misinterpret the actions of others from time to time and this might lead to behaviour that appears to be sexually motivated. An example of this is a man who has an erection triggered by intimate touching by the careworker while showering him or as a result of a general misunderstanding of and confusion about a careworker's words and actions.

Mistaking others

Inability to recognise or remember people and place them correctly in their lives can, particularly in residential care, lead a person to a liaison with a stranger which may or may not have a sexual component. Partnerships and liaisons of this type are discussed in detail in chapter 8.

Sexual fantasies

Sexual therapists say that most of us indulge in fantasies during sexual play and sexual intercourse, and that these fantasies contribute to a healthy sex life. From time to time we hear of someone with dementia who indulges in a fantasy or has a delusion or hallucination that has a sexual content. One man said that his sexual fantasies during intercourse had become more erotic since he was affected by dementia and this had greatly enhanced the pleasure of making love for both his wife and himself.

How much or how many people with dementia fantasise about things sexual, or how sexual fantasy affects their behaviour, is hard to assess mainly because of the difficulty in communicating with them at this level. In any event, it is only if sexual fantasising

The catastrophic reaction

The nature of the catastrophic reaction is often misunderstood, sometimes used synonymously with sudden violent behaviour in people with dementia. This is not the full picture.

The catastrophic theory, originally applied in biological science, has been adapted to a number of other disciplines, including aspects of human behaviour. Put simply it means that certain catastrophic events or stimuli will trigger a change in the way that a person acts.

When treating brain-damaged patients, a Dr Goldstein earlier this century found that when he presented them with a task or a memory that was too much for them, they would be overwhelmed, and anxiety and irritability flooded over them. They coped with these feelings with inappropriate and excessive emotions and behaviours. These took the form of restlessness, agitation, hyperactivity, anger, tremor, tears, determined refusal to cooperate or evasiveness (evasiveness can take the form of physical avoidance or emotional withdrawal). It was something like a panic attack.

Common catastrophic reactions of the person with dementia include frantic pacing, agitated and night wandering, aggression, crying, whimpering and hysterics, determined non-cooperation and emotional withdrawal. Of course these sorts of behaviours can happen for other reasons too, but it is the reason for the behaviour happening that separates a catastrophic reaction from other emotional or behavioural reactions.

It is important to understand the catastrophic reaction, because we often unwittingly precipitate this reaction in people with dementia. Catastrophic reactions are less likely to happen if we avoid:

- presenting a task that is too difficult
- recalling distressing memories
- making sudden or unnecessary changes
- applying physical restraint
- arguing or unduly insisting or reasoning.

interferes with their own well-being or the lives of those around them, that we need or have a right to know.

The woman who believes she is pregnant because her abdomen is swollen with age is a common fantasy. Sometimes this is embroidered further when she imagines she has been raped or that the father of her 'child' is some young man in the family, or a friend. Problems can arise when she acts out this fantasy.

Mrs Knox appeared at breakfast one morning distraught, repeating over and over that she had been raped. Because of her level of distress and the incoherence of what she was trying to tell them, staff at the nursing home could only elicit garbled details of the attack. The administration was involved, police were called, staff counselled and extra security measures put in place. It was only after a medical examination, which showed no trace of intercourse, that her story was doubted. After some weeks of painstaking 'discussion', the counsellor unwound her story. Mrs Knox had put on a lot of weight and one day, apparently catching sight of her naked body in the bathroom mirror, she had fantasised a pregnancy. She had already been 'daydreaming' for some weeks that an unknown young man was having sex with her. Eventually the anxiety of her secret overcame her and she blurted out the story about the rape. The relief of having an understanding listener lessened her anxiety about being raped and she soon stopped talking about it. The fantasy about her 'pregnancy' persisted for some time, but her insistence that she was 'having a baby' lessened, firstly when staff stopped mocking her and secondly, as her dementia worsened.

Staff in one dementia-specific unit found that by playing along with such a fantasy they were able to smooth the anxiety exhibited by other residents and by the woman involved. They sympathised with the woman's 'morning sickness' (after ascertaining that there was no medical reason for her complaints) and gave her extra care and attention. Some of the careworkers even started a baby trousseau for her, bringing in unwanted baby clothes which she lovingly stored in her cupboard. The significant outcome of handling 'the pregnancy' in this way was the obvious pleasure the woman displayed as a result of the attentive and caring attitude of staff, and that she stopped worrying other residents.

When behaviour is out of control

One of the functions of the frontal lobes of the brain is to monitor the appropriateness of the way we act and modify and control behaviour. When this part of the brain is affected, the capacity to distinguish between actions that are appropriate and those which are not is gradually lost. The person will have difficulty in distinguishing between the 'right way' and the 'wrong way' to behave. This is called disinhibited behaviour.

Disinhibited behaviour

The person who behaves in a disinhibited way is sometimes said to have lost social control or to have lost all inhibitions. To gain some understanding of disinhibited sexual actions, we need to look at the nature of sexual behaviour.

Sex is a very strong physical urge. It is one of three primitive or in-built drives that are part of the make-up of all animals, including humans; the other two drives being hunger and self-protection. You may hear these drives also referred to as instincts or the sexual drive called the libido. All three are instinctively aimed at survival: hunger and self-protection enhance personal survival, while sex is associated with procreation and population: survival of a species. If our hunger is satisfied and our safety ensured, sex or the libido can become the strongest of the three drives with the added appeal of being pleasurable.

What sets us humans apart from other animals is that we have learned from a very early age to control our primitive drives. Through our moral training we develop mechanisms or inhibitions that are stored in the frontal lobes of the brain and which perform the function of restraining our in-built desires and channelling them into more socially acceptable behaviour. Even so, it is not unusual for people to experience conflict between their basic sexual desires and learned control. Fortunately most of us are able to think through this dilemma with restraint usually winning. It is only when our control mechanisms break down that basic impulses are unleashed. When this happens, the ways in which we act are often not appropriate or acceptable to other people.

When a person is affected with dementia and the parts of the brain that store up inhibitions are damaged, behaviour invariably becomes uncontrolled. You might notice that someone with dementia will stuff their mouths with food, often picking up large handfuls, even though they may not be hungry. Others will hit out quite violently at a threat to their person, when none exists. Sometimes when control breaks down, behaviours can be sexually indecent in the extreme and at worst can severely shock or at best cause embarrassment to others.

> The members of a religious order were startled to hear one of their more senior members shouting a string of lewd and sexually explicit phrases at mealtime. There was no explanation as to how she could have heard these words, given that she came from a strict background and had spent all her adult life as a respected member of a closed order. Shortly afterwards, she was diagnosed with a dementia and foul language characterised her behaviour for some time.

Aware but out of control

In most instances of disinhibited behaviour the person does not realise that the behaviour is inappropriate. Occasionally, however, someone will know that what they have done is unacceptable. This awareness of the nature of the behaviour is more likely to happen in the earlier stages of dementia, and even though the person recognises that the way they have behaved is unacceptable, there is a helplessness in exercising control when a similar impulse overtakes them. The anxiety that may be experienced in such cases can be eased by the reassurance that someone will be there to help control this behaviour.

During the morning at the day club, a tearful Bruce confided to the supervisor that he had 'assaulted' his friend. Bruce lived at home with his wife and, even though he was still fairly independent, had some difficulty in finding his way around and was unable to go out alone. A teenage daughter of a lifelong friend of Bruce's family, came every so often to sit with him to give his wife time out. The day before, while she was reading to him, he had reached out, put his hand into her blouse and touched her breast. He remembered that the young woman had thrown down the book and rushed out of the room. Bruce said to the supervisor, 'I don't know what made me do it. I feel so ashamed. I know she'll never want to see me again, and my wife'll be so angry when she finds out.' Fortunately, there was a fairly satisfactory resolution to this incident. Both families understood the difficulties associated with dementia behaviour, and the young woman realised that not only had she been wearing a low-cut, see-through blouse, but also that she had been leaning over him.

This is examined in more detail in chapter 6 as an example of the problem solving approach.

Previous behaviour

Much of the behaviour associated with dementia is recognisable as a carry over from the way the person acted before they were affected. Even though it might be distorted or exaggerated, it bears strong traces of more 'normal' behaviour.

Philippa, the worker in charge of the dementia section of a small nursing home, complained of the lecherous nature of one of the men in her care. 'He isn't content with the women here', she said, 'he's always after women in other sections — can't keep his hands off every woman he meets'. She was so disapproving of his behaviour that it was all she could do to talk to him, let alone treat him kindly. What made her even angrier was that he seemed to have a happy family; his wife visited most days and his sons and daughters visited regularly. The wife eventually provided an explanation for her husband's behaviour. A war veteran, he had for many years been a Legatee, responsible for the welfare of soldiers' widows and children, and many of the women he visited were well known to him. The fact that he occasionally held the hand of a resident or visited a woman he did not previously know, did not appear to upset any of them. He was simply pursuing a behaviour that was familiar to himself and to most of the women he visited.

This situation is discussed in more detail in chapter 6 as an example of the problem solving approach.

Meeting needs

Dementia robs people of their identity, confidence and self-esteem; consequently they may not know who they really are or where they fit in the world and with the people around them. The nature and quality of family relationships and friendships change, in some instances disintegrating altogether and leaving the person without close support. In such cases, professional carers, volunteers and community visitors have some responsibility to meet the needs for affection of the socially isolated person. It is in this sort of circumstance that a clear understanding of a careworker's intentions becomes paramount so that a professionally supportive relationship does not get out of control. In particular this is so when the worker and client or resident are of the opposite gender.

Ninety-year-old Joseph who lived alone and was apparently without family and friends was visited by a home respite worker twice weekly. From her first contact some eighteen months before, she reacted to what she saw as his loneliness and craving for affection. She treated him in the way she responded to her grandfather; an arm around his shoulder, a squeeze of the hand, a hug, sharing a joke and an occasional kiss on the withered cheek. Over time Joseph became more confident and returned the affection — from not letting go of her hand to trying an intimate embrace. She wriggled free, withdrew her hand and generally made fun of the incidents, chiding him for being 'a bit of a flirt', nevertheless she felt more than a little uncomfortable. Then one day, either having lost all inhibition because of his advancing dementia, or encouraged by her manner, or even mistaking the nature of the relationship, he asked her directly for genital sex. She left.

It is difficult not to respond with affection to a frail old person, alone and lonely, particularly when there is a positive response to the careworker's attention. However, letting situations get out of hand will often result in distress for the careworker and deprivation for the client. In this case, it would have been better had the worker restricted her attentions to less physical contact and relied more on a caring demeanour, with occasional hand-holding and a friendly hug. The parameters of the careworker–client relationship need to be clearly communicated either verbally or non-verbally to the person with dementia in whichever way and at whatever level can be understood and these boundaries may need to be continually redrawn.

Similar situations can be encountered in a nursing home or hostel where residents are dependent on staff to meet their needs for affection. It is more likely however, that the intensity of a relationship of any intimacy will be diluted by the number of staff, shift changes and staff supervision.

Sexual components of problem situations

When assessing a general problem situation, a sexual component is often overlooked as a contributing factor. It may well be that what lies behind the behaviour is a need for affection or a frustration at sexual needs not being met.

In one nursing home an occupational therapist assessing the extreme agitation and snappiness of a woman before bedtime, observed that at this time of the evening she gravitated towards a picture of a rock star in the dining-room. The woman crooned to the picture, stroked and kissed the face. Sensing that the woman's behaviour was associated with desire for an intimate relationship, the therapist arranged for her to have a 'cuddling' pillow in her bed at night and encouraged staff to give her more hugs. Her agitation and night wandering ceased.

Some facts about dementia

There are over 100 causes of dementia. The main types are dementia of the Alzheimer's type and vascular dementia.

Dementia is not a normal part of ageing. However, people are more at risk of developing dementia in old age in the same way that they are more likely to suffer from heart disease, arthritis and cancer. Dementia can also occur at a much younger age; the first person diagnosed by Dr Alzheimer in 1906 was 56. The chance of dementia occurring increases with age, from a little over one in 100 people aged 60–69 years to one in four people aged over 80. Because the world's aged population is increasing, the incidence of dementia is expected to rise dramatically over the next twenty years.

Depression in old age is a common condition. As it symptoms are similar to those of dementia in the early stages, it is possible for one to be mistaken for the other. The symptoms of depression are treatable if medical advice is sought for a proper diagnosis. A person with dementia can also become depressed.

People with dementia will behave in different ways, depending on the area of the brain affected and the extent of the underlying damage. Actions often appear to be irrational. Difficulties in understanding, following instructions and carrying on a rational conversation are common. Usually people with dementia are not able to control or change their behaviour, except in some instances where they can with help modify certain actions.

CHAPTER
5

Problems of
sexually charged
behaviour

As already discussed, impaired capacity to modify, change or restrain their actions may lead to dementia-affected people behaving oddly and acting in ways that are disruptive and seem to be out of control. If this behaviour is associated with sexuality it can at times cause great embarrassment and emotional distress to relatives and friends. Service providers as well as families are invariably at a loss to know the best way to respond.

Home vs residential care

The sort of behaviour that creates problems in the home can also cause situations that are difficult to cope with in a nursing home or dementia hostel. But there are differences. In residential care there are many more episodes of sexually embarrassing and undesirable sexual activity to be dealt with and more behaviours with a sexual component, simply because of the number of people living together in one place. Behaviour may develop in residential care that was not evident in the person's home. Several reasons have been suggested for this such as heightened confusion due to a change of lifestyle and living among strangers in an unfamiliar place. Within this framework there will also be stimuli that did not exist in the home environment which will act as triggers for new behaviour. It may also be the case that actions judged as sexually motivated or indecent in residential care would be considered normal in the person's own home.

> In her home fifty-four-year old Lois wandered from bathroom to bedroom either without clothes or covering only the lower half of her body with a towel. When she continued wandering naked in her room in the dementia unit with the door open, despite being directed not to do so, staff judged this behaviour to be deliberate, labelling it as sexual exposure or indecent. This situation was further complicated for Lois by the variety of ways in which staff reacted to her behaviour from gentle correction to shocked disapproval and embarrassed mirth.

Different perspectives

Even when the behaviour in residential care is similar to that in the home, there can be marked differences in the way that actions are perceived and handled.

> Unlike Lois, Mr Bennett had always been most circumspect in his manner of dress and discreet in his behaviour. One day he wandered down the garden path and through the front gate to visit the next door neighbours. There was nothing unusual about this, except that he was dressed only in his old straw hat, underpants and slippers. His neighbour quickly ushered him inside, covered him with her dressing gown and phoned Mrs Bennett. Without a fuss, they dressed him together. He never attempted to do this again, but just in case, his wife made sure he was properly dressed at all times.

The manner in which this episode was handled is an example of the way a neighbourhood can respond to a family's dilemma when they understand and accept the person with dementia. Early in Mr

Bennett's diagnosis with Alzheimer's disease, his wife had alerted her neighbours to changes that might take place in his behaviour as well as discussing the effects that it would have on his independence.

A different sort of relationship

The way in which behaviour is perceived and treated in the home and in residential care is influenced by the different nature of the relationship that the family and the careworker have with the affected person. The person with dementia is 'mother', 'father', 'husband', 'wife', or 'partner', bonded to family members with all the historical and emotional ties of that relationship. Sexual ties, taboos and boundaries are embodied in the emotional life of a family, elements of which will remain with the members for as long as the person with dementia is alive. Reactions to the sexual behaviour of the affected person will depend on the nature of the kinship ties and on the climate of the family relationship at any given time. The professional worker, particularly the residential careworker, maintains a working rather than a friendship or kinship relationship with the person with dementia, and in most cases is limited to dealing with the situation of the moment. When he or she walks out of the door and leaves the resident–worker relationship and the day's work behind the careworker is relieved of the pressure of any problem that has arisen.

Does sexuality have to be a problem?

Have you noticed how many times the words 'problem' or 'challenging behaviour' burst into the conversation when the topic of sex and dementia comes up in discussion among professional carers? It is almost as though the very existence of sexuality in people with dementia is in itself a problem. Part of the reason for this must be due to misunderstanding the sexuality of older people and a denial of the existence of their sexual needs. Could it also be that service providers are now taught to be 'challenged' by the behaviour of older people in their care and to 'manage' them rather than develop an understanding and a way of responding to their actions? Do they at times feel compelled to see as a 'challenge' any behaviour that does not fit in with their personal expectations, or consider an action to be a problem if the dementia-affected person acts in a way that does not conform to a prescribed pattern? To see a problem where none may exist? That was the situation with Mr Jackson (see page 69).

Complexity of sexual behaviour

The issue of sexuality and dementia is a very grey area and, because of its complexity, the designing of guidelines for professional carer response is difficult in the extreme. What is the difference between sexual behaviour and immoral behaviour? Whose responsibility is it to handle or make decisions about sexual behaviour in residential care? What is the legal liability of the service provider? How much behaviour of an explicit nature should residential careworkers or the respite worker in the home be expected to put up with? What rights of sexual expression does the person with dementia have? How is choice determined? What constitutes consent?

Do professional carers have the right to enquire into the sexual activity of married couples? Should families confide in service providers about 'abnormal' sexual behaviour? Should residential care staff advise the family of a sexual problem? How would the media react to the knowledge that a facility allowed, let alone encouraged, residents to have a sex life? The maze of questions and doubts are endless and the answers complex. Some of these issues are discussed at length in chapters 9 and 10.

Interpretation of behaviour

Dementia behaviour is seldom logical so often there is not a direct connection between cause and effect or reason and consequence of a person's actions. A behaviour that we interpret as sexual may not have any association with sexuality at all. In assessing any piece of dementia behaviour and when looking for reasons and motivation for it, it is necessary to go beyond the obvious signs.

Is the action sexually motivated?

Is the woman removing her clothing in public or the man who walks out of the front gate clad only in a singlet engaging in sexual exposure? Invariably not. Undressing is normal behaviour; most of us undress at least once every day. Heat, discomfort and boredom are common stimuli for someone with dementia to remove clothing and the ability to stop once the behaviour has started is probably impaired; the knowledge that 'you don't do that here' has been lost. It is the place that is inappropriate, not the behaviour. The man who masturbates or urinates in public is often believed to have some sexual motivation, whereas this may not be so at all. Consider alternatives! A urinary tract infection may be the underlying cause. The trigger may be something as simple as wanting to relieve a full bladder and being unaware that this is not the place to do so. The person accused of approaching another for sexual purposes may be merely reaching out for companionship.

When the action is sexually motivated

The type of behaviour that is aimed towards sexual gratification often creates more serious problems for families and careworkers and is invariably more difficult to deal with than that behaviour which is otherwise motivated.

One of the first factors to consider in making an assessment of any dementia behaviour is whether or not the actions we are judging as abnormal have been part and parcel of the person's previous lifestyle. The behaviour of the sexually aggressive person may indeed be a carry over from a time before the dementia took hold. Only the circumstances are different. We have to ask if the behaviour is characteristic of the person's previous way of life. What is being judged as an increased sex drive may not be that at all. The person may well have had a habitually high need for sexual gratification. The man who indiscriminately harasses women may

have always been something of a woman chaser, but before dementia he would have been more careful about the 'where' and the 'who
with'. The woman who was a sex worker in her younger days may
try to renew a long since abandoned profession when she becomes
affected by dementia.

> It seemed fairly obvious that frail seventy-year-old Ms Lily Whyte
> had begun to relive her heyday as one of the 'girls' in the
> upmarket hotel in Kings Cross during the Vietnam War. A day or
> two after she came to the nursing home for two weeks' respite
> while her male carer was on holiday, she had an unusual number
> of male visitors who she entertained in her bedroom. Not only
> had she brought her 'clientele' with her but acquired new
> 'customers' from the male residents there. By the time the
> management committee dealt with the staff's request to have
> her transferred, it was time for her to return home.

The fact that a behaviour was part of the normal way of life for
someone before they were afflicted with dementia, does not imply
that we have to approve of it, but it does add to our understanding. But understanding or not, if and when the way the person
manifests his or her sexuality causes serious problems for carers
and fear in others in a nursing home or hostel, some means has to
be found to deal with the situation.

When needs for sexual gratification are aggressively pursued
either through demands on others or actions of self-expressed intimacy, a number of physical and psychological factors need to be
taken into account before any plan of action is contemplated. Is
the behaviour due to the effects of damage to the brain? Is there an
element of intent? Certain prescribed medications can heighten
sexual desire or hormonal levels can add to sexual tension.
Someone who is deprived of a satisfying sexual relationship with
a partner, either through distance or death, may experience a good
deal of sexual frustration and aggressively seek gratification.

Triggers for sexual conduct

Misunderstanding another's actions and intentions is a common and often powerful trigger for sexually charged behaviour by a person with dementia. Even the closeness or touch of a careworker when the dementing person is being undressed or showered can stimulate sexual desire. Erections are not uncommon during tasks of intimate caring and on occasions responses may be sexually explicit or the person will act in a sexually aggressive way towards the careworker.

Sometimes a careworker report suggests that there could be a 'retaliation' motive in some sexual behaviour especially when it is aggressive or indecent:

> Every time I came near Ray he let fly with a string of dirty words. When I showered him, he'd masturbate. One time he urinated on my foot and he wasn't past fondling his private parts or opening his fly when I was [near him] in the dining-room. I loved my work [in the dementia unit], but he only did this with me. I thought if this went on much longer I was going to have to leave. Anyway, after thinking about it I decided to see the nursing home's social worker ... I discovered that I really had an attitude about this man. He reminded me of an old man who lived near me at home, who used to [expose himself] to all the kids on our way home from school. And I'd really been treating this old guy roughly, shouting at him and one day I'd pushed him ... Anyway [after this] I began to talk to him and do little things for him like cut his fingernails and talk about the people in his photos and he seemed to understand that I'd changed my attitude and he didn't do those horrible things any more.

Other than touch, little attention is accorded to the role that sensory stimulation plays in explicit sexual behaviour of the person with dementia. Smell, sight and sound, alone or in combination with other stimuli, can and do act as triggers for sexual actions.

Every time eighty-year-old Mr Trent found himself in the company of the male day centre supervisor he made sexual overtures to him even though the supervisor was not homosexual. Not only did the supervisor bear some physical resemblance to Mr Trent's life-long partner when young, but he also used the same aftershave lotion and, like the partner, was a violinist. When this information about Mr Trent's background became known, as well as firmly discouraging the man's advances, the supervisor changed his brand of aftershave and stopped playing the violin on the days Mr Trent attended. The advances gradually decreased.

Common problem situations

Areas where problems of sexuality are most likely to occur with people with dementia fall into five broad groups:
- sexual modesty
- specific behaviours
- changes in sexual patterns in marriage
- effects of behaviour changes on family members
- illicit relationships.

We have already discussed sexual modesty of older people. Here we examine specific behaviours that create difficulties for carers and others.

Specific behaviours

The sorts of behaviours that commonly create problems are:
- indiscreet behaviour
- sexually explicit actions such as public exposure, self-fondling, masturbation and urination
- obscene or sexually explicit language
- harassment – touching, fondling, indecent approaches. (Note that all of the above can be harassment depending on the intent of the perpetrator and the perception of the receiver.)

Indiscreet behaviour

The type of incident referred to here is one that may occur only once or twice and involves only a suggestion of sexuality: a hug or a kiss that is a little more than friendly, a lewd joke, or the occasional use of indecent language. These 'minor' actions happen with a number of people with dementia but may be so infrequent or mild that they go unnoticed. These sorts of indiscretions are generally inoffensive, or otherwise reasonably acceptable to others, particularly when the nature of dementia and its effect on the afflicted person is understood. However, in designating the behaviours as minor, I fully recognise that the depth of embarrassment experienced varies from person to person and will depend on the circumstances in which the behaviour occurs. I do not underestimate the often traumatic effect that these 'indiscretions' may have on both professional and family carers.

> Mrs Snell showed a childlike affection for everybody including her family, the staff of the nursing home where she lived, other residents and the large doll from which she was inseparable, continually planting dribbly kisses on all of them. Occasionally she sat on the couch, encircling a surprised male resident in a fond embrace. She was not persistent and withdrew immediately people rebuffed her attentions. Staff found that by gently extricating her from her more intimate overtures and returning her demonstrations of affection she remained content and cooperative.

Sometimes a spontaneous behaviour will startle onlookers and leave the humiliated carer at a loss for words.

> It was the evening of Sandra Cox's pre-wedding party and most of the guests had arrived when Mr Cox appeared on the balcony at the top of the stairs calling to his wife that he could not find his shirt. Shocked and red-faced guests could not help but notice that he was dressed only in singlet and socks and one elderly couple quickly left. Sandra said she was disgusted and ashamed

by her father's behaviour and devastated by the degree of humiliation her mother was suffering. There was added discomfort in having to announce on that special occasion that Mr Cox had recently been diagnosed with Pick's disease. Most of the guests understood and sympathised with the family. While Mr Cox remained at home, this behaviour did not occur again, but briefly re-emerged in his early days in a dementia hostel.

Sexually explicit behaviour

Included in this group of behaviours is urinating in public, sexual exposure and self-expressed intimacy such as masturbating and self-fondling. Carers usually find the behaviour distasteful and unpleasant.

On occasions the behaviour appears to be deliberate because of the intensity with which it is presented and the circumstances in which it happens. But this is by no means always the case, it may be as a consequence of the dementia. Sometimes the behaviour can be modified, but if it is associated with specific brain damage it is likely to return and the modifying technique will have to be reapplied each time.

Urinating in public

When this happens, it is usually, although not exclusively, in the more advanced stages of the dementia and is often judged to be sexually motivated. This is probably because, when the person urinating is male, the penis is exposed. In one dementia unit a woman appeared to have some sexual desire in the company of a certain man and she would squat beside him and urinate through her clothes. By removing the trigger, the man, to another section of the unit, the behaviour stopped. However, this sort of incident appears to be rare.

Often the trigger for urination is purely physical; the person has the urge to relieve a full bladder and either cannot find the way to the toilet or is not aware any more that the toilet is the place to go. Another common trigger is the presence of a utensil that is similarly shaped to a toilet bowl such as a waste paper basked or a pot plant. Even a cardboard box has been known to stimulate a person to urinate. One family found that the only way it could deal with this was to replace all basketware and other absorbent utensils with those made of plastic, which were easier to clean and reusable. There has been some success in modifying this type of behaviour by training the person to respond to orientation cues. However, unless they are really obvious, cues or signposts are not usually sufficient in themselves for people with dementia even though for some – and only some – a picture of a toilet on the toilet door can be effective. The person has to be taught to use the cues. For example, the researchers Bird, Alexopoulos and Adamowicz (1995) used a memory technique called spaced retrieval to help an eighty-three-year-old man they called 'Max'.

> Max's habit of urinating in the corners of rooms was of such concern to his family that they were about to ask for him to be admitted to a nursing home. Accordingly, in two 1-hour sessions, Max was taught to associate a large coloured sign with the location of the toilet by repeatedly testing his memory for the meaning of the sign, over gradually increasing intervals. Occasional prompting from his family remained necessary, especially at night, but Max's voiding behaviour ceased to be a problem and he was able to remain at home for four more months.

Continuity and constancy of response are essential if this technique is to be effective; everybody involved must respond uniformly. Each case has its own specific elements, so before embarking on this technique with any person or behaviour an in-depth assessment is necessary. The application of the spaced retrieval technique can be complicated, and consultation with a psychologist or other professional familiar with the technique is recommended.

Masturbating in public

This is an activity of both men and women, but more likely to be manifested in public by men. Self-expressed intimacy such as masturbation is more often than not judged to be sexually charged. This is indeed sometimes the case and is a carry over from the way the person has always achieved sexual gratification. However, other triggers have to be considered to understand such behaviour: boredom, urgency to relieve bladder or bowel, discomfort due to tight clothing or a reaction to high temperature.

Beryl had probably been in the habit of masturbating all of her adult life, but nobody noticed her behaving in this way in the hostel until a couch appeared in the recreation room. The couch was a magnet. Every time Beryl came into the room, she shooed the occupants away, lay down, pulled up her clothes and masturbated. Eventually the couch was moved back to the nursing home section, and Beryl confined her pleasure to her own bed.

When masturbating and genital fondling are a habitual way of relieving sexual tension, a place should be provided where the person can indulge his or her sexual need with some dignity. Scolding or mocking is never to be tolerated. If the behaviour takes place publicly, then the person should be quietly escorted to a bedroom or some other place where they can carry on in privacy. In nursing homes women residents are often shocked to the point of hysteria when a man masturbates in public and male residents can be loud in their condemnation. A quiet explanation that the person does not know where he is and is not doing this on purpose will often reassure them, but the same explanation may have to be repeated whenever the same incident occurs.

Some careworkers report incidents where masturbating appears to be a deliberate attempt to sexually harass; sometimes as an overture or invitation for sex with a particular person.

For some eighteen months, ever since he had arrived at the dementia unit, Mr Snell had occasionally masturbated and fondled his genitals and at times deliberately exposed his penis. When a new personal care assistant was appointed to the unit,

The story of masturbation

Over the centuries the practice of masturbation has caused more controversy than probably any other matter related to sexuality; periodically designated as sinful, indecent and self-abusive and more recently as contributing to and sometimes necessary for sexual health and well-being. According to Rabbi Brasch in his book *How Did Sex Begin?* male masturbation was once practised as a religious duty. In pagan worship men masturbated to enable semen to be offered to the gods as a sacrifice in order for them to maintain the world and its fertility. Among primitive peoples male masturbation was considered to be 'normal' and desirable at some stages of life such as adolescence. A major shift in beliefs about masturbation came with the Judaeo–Christian tradition, when authorities were determined to distance themselves as far as possible from paganism and pagan customs. So ancient rites and practices were declared to be sinful and the rituals that had served societies in the past were outlawed, including the practice of masturbation.

When people finally made the connection between sperm and procreation, male masturbation was considered to be an undesirable practice. The reason for this was the belief that it wasted the means of begetting children and so would decrease the potential for increasing the population and strength of a particular society. So this behaviour that had once served ancient communities well became a capital offence. A crime. A man could be put to death if he was caught. Over time there was a gradual shift from a strictly societal and legal stance to one of health risk and morality. A whole heap of mythology grew up around masturbation. Parents were warned about the evils of self-abuse for their male children. It was impressed on them that the offender would become blind, sterile or mad. Or if they were ever capable of fathering a child it would surely be born weak and disabled. Or some other awful disaster would befall it.

These myths gathered remarkable acceptance over the ages, long after medical science knew that there was no health risk. It was not biologically possible for these things to happen as a consequence of masturbation. But even today this mythology persists in some quarters, creating a lot of fear and shame and guilt with sometimes far-reaching effects on people's intimate relationships.

Mutual masturbation is a major element of sexual activity for many sexual partners and adds to the overall enjoyment of intercourse. Modern day authorities emphasise the positive contribution that masturbation can make to the physical and psychological health of both men and women who feel comfortable in its use.

he targeted her for this behaviour and pursued her, increasing the frequency of exposure and masturbation. Despite many attempts to modify the behaviour, it increased in frequency and intensity. The personal care assistant left. However, the behaviour continued and Mr Snell became increasingly more aggressive in his demands for sex from most of the female staff. Eventually the prescribing of a testosterone-inhibiting medication modified his behaviour to a point where it was manageable.

Among techniques suggested for controlling self-expressed sexual behaviour such as masturbation, self-fondling, and sexual exposure are physical restraints of various types. However, I believe that physical restraint of any type should only be applied as a very last measure and after every other type of response has been canvassed. The use of restraint can create more problems than it solves.

Sexual harassment

This sort of sexually aggressive behaviour is more commonly associated with men than with women, but women can also harass others in a sexually explicit way. Occurrences of sexual harassment are not unknown in the home but are much more likely to take place in residential care. Why is this so? For men is it the proximity of a number of mostly young female staff or easy access to female residents? Or in the case of homosexual people the proximity of other males and male staff? Is it a carry over from a person's usual lifestyle? Perhaps it is a misunderstanding of the actions of staff or residents. Or a reaction to provocation. Until researchers throw some light on it and why there is a variation in behaviour between home and residential care, in practice we have to rely on trial and error in responding to types of behaviour and on evaluating the outcome of various responses.

We also have to accept that in some situations the harassing behaviour has a strong and deliberate element of intent.

Alexopoulos (1994) reported on an eighty-seven-year old man, Mr E, with vascular dementia who had lived for four and a half years in a psychiatric institution. Women patients had complained of inappropriate touching and his sexually disinhibited behaviour was the reason for his continuing care in the psychiatric hospital rather than a nursing home. The spaced retrieval technique was applied to his behaviour. In the learning and eventual successful carrying out of a ward rule designed for the occasion — No touching any females on the ward — there seemed to be a suggestion that Mr E was well aware of his harassment of the women in that there was some deliberate reluctance to relinquish his behaviour. This is further evidenced by his comments, 'Who made up this rule anyway?' and 'It will never work'.

Staff harassment
Sexually harassing behaviour can be difficult to respond to, modify or control and gentle care, best intentions and quality professional inputs can all fail.

Staff of a large nursing home were all apprehensive about caring for Mr X. He constantly made deliberate and explicit requests for sex, fondling the breasts of female staff and reaching under their skirts when they came close; calling them ladies of the night and using obscene language. His pleasure was obvious and when they became distressed it seemed to urge him on to greater obscenities. A medical examination did not disclose any physical abnormality or irritating conditions that would contribute to the behaviour. Various attempts were made to modify the behaviour. A program of distractions, using activities which interested him was tried and behavioural specialists designed an intensive modification program. All without success. Two of the factors seen as contributing to the failure of the programs were the strength of the motivation for Mr X's behaviour and the disinclination of some staff to cooperate with the steps suggested, so that there was no uniformity of response. Staff presented a petition to the administration of the organisation asking to have Mr X transferred to a psychiatric institution or another facility more able to deal with serious deviant behaviour. The request was refused on the grounds that the organisation had a duty of care to look after all residents.

This brings up the issue of the rights of workers. How much harassment should careworkers be expected to tolerate? How do we balance the rights of careworkers with the rights of residents? This is further discussed in chapter 10.

Harassment of other residents

The will of staff to control the behaviour of the person who harasses other residents is seldom in doubt, with residential care staff accepting without question the duty of care to protect residents from harm. If we take the case of Mr X, it was only when he turned his attentions to two women residents that the board of management agreed for him to be transferred to a psychiatric facility for treatment. There he was prescribed medication in sufficient strength to dampen his sexual drive to the extent where he showed little interest in the opposite sex. He returned to the nursing home.

The effectiveness of using a sex worker as part of the response strategy when dealing with severe sexual harassment is becoming increasingly recognised. Some facilities have reported successful outcomes in cases where a male harasser had been known to previously patronise prostitutes. On a more altruistic level, one nursing home used a sex worker to relieve the extreme sexual frustration of one of its male residents.

Room-hopping

Where residents are mobile, wandering into somebody else's room and lying on the bed is not unusual. Women are particularly resentful of this sort of behaviour and are annoyed at their private space being invaded. If the intruder is a man and he happens to lie down beside her, or undresses in her presence, the woman will invariably attach some sexual motive to his actions. She feels that she is being 'propositioned' or about to be attacked. What often follows is great anxiety about the fear of sexual attack, not only in her own room, but whenever the intruding person appears or sits near her in a public place. This fear is exacerbated if the man displays signs of insistence or aggression. If the occupant of the room being invaded is chairbound, her anxiety is heightened by her feeling of helplessness.

Staff in one special hostel had some success in persuading the women to report such an incident immediately, so that they could lead the intruder away and divert his attention. The women were assured that the intruder meant no harm and that because of his 'sickness' he was unable to control his wandering. This message was repeated every time there was an 'invasion'. Some of the women were able to learn to shut their doors when occupying their rooms and others 'protected' those who were unable to comprehend staff reassurances. Staff found that the women's anxiety decreased and their abusive attitude towards the intruder modified. In one purpose-built unit stable doors were fitted, so that when the residents were occupying rooms they were able to learn to lock the lower half of the door by sliding the latch, preventing unwanted visitors but still feeling part of the outside activity.

In the majority of cases, there does not appear to be any sexual intent in this sort of behaviour, rather it is the sight of the bed that acts as a prompt for the wanderer to lie down. The difficulty comes in convincing a frightened women of this, especially if she is lying on the bed at the time. While this behaviour seems to be associated with men who wander rather than women, female 'invaders' are also common although they do not seem to constitute a sexual threat, but rather an irritation.

CHAPTER

6

Solving the problem

It is patently clear to most family carers and service providers that there is no one effective way of dealing with all dementia behaviours or even a single way of responding to any one behaviour. There is no single solution either; one problem behaviour might be surprisingly simple to deal with, whereas other circumstances can be extremely complex and the resolution difficult. This is understandable given the interweaving of so many factors – pathological, psychological and environmental – in dementia behaviour.

Various techniques have achieved some degree of success: distraction and diversion, strong and continuous disapproval, reward and praise, medication, the provision of a warm caring atmosphere with a minimum of negative stimuli and the spaced retrieval technique. The problem solving approach offers another valuable technique for responding to a behaviour that is causing difficulties, in particular when the contributing factors are environmental or interpersonal. And because it seeks to find and modify the reason for the behaviour, there is a good chance of the effect lasting.

The problem solving approach

When we focus solely on a person's behaviour what we are trying to fix can be simply a symptom of a larger underlying problem so the behaviour simply doesn't get any better or, if modified, soon recurs. Instead of targeting a behaviour, the problem solving approach (Sherman, 1994) deals with the whole situation. It looks at a network of factors: the circumstances that contribute to the problem, the interaction of everyone involved and the consequences of these dynamics.

The problem solving approach can be likened to a photographic shoot where the camera operator uses a wide angle lens to include background, scenery and people as well as the main subject in the photograph. The problem solving approach broadens the focus to take in the whole scenario and all of the players. As well as assessing the dynamics of the total situation, this method also avoids the pitfall of laying blame on resident, staff or family which can happen when we look at undesirable or 'challenging' behaviour.

Planning the problem solving approach

There are three aspects involved in the problem solving approach:
- defining the problem
- assessing the person in the situation
- planning a strategy to solve the problem.

These three aspects are interactive rather than sequential. As more information about the problem comes to light and responses are evaluated, strategies may need to be modified and the problem reworked.

Defining the problem

What is the problem? Is it the behaviour of the person with dementia? Is it the attitude of other residents? Is it a family problem?

Whose problem is it? Is it a problem for everyone – staff and family – or just one person? Sometimes we label a certain behaviour a problem because it does not conform to our beliefs, attitudes and the proper way to act or because we find it uncomfortable or difficult to handle. But these are our problems and not necessarily problems for others, or for the person with dementia. We may be the solution to the problem.

What is the desirable outcome? What would be the very best

outcome? Without doubt the most desirable outcome for the man who masturbates in public would be for him to cease this sort of exposure.

What is a tolerable outcome? Of course we would all like to achieve the perfect outcome, but this is not always possible. So consider an outcome with which everybody concerned will be reasonably satisfied, for example, decrease the frequency of masturbation in public places. Tolerable outcomes are much more likely to be achieved and so give some feeling of success.

At the end of *Defining the problem*, we now have an overview of the problem and a clear objective to work towards.

Assessing the person in the situation

Ask what is happening to make this a problem. This next step is to assess the person, together with all the factors that may be contributing to the problem. We are now looking for the core of the problem and the circumstances that trigger the behaviour.

The person

Problem behaviour can be directly associated with physical or psychiatric factors. Do not overlook these.

Assess if the person is:

- unwell, in pain, uncomfortable
- overtired, overstimulated, bored, anxious, frustrated
- embarrassed, ignored, misunderstood, feeling patronised
- delusional, hallucinatory, depressed.

Assess if the person is reacting to:

- an unpleasant incident or association, or change
- a memory
- provocation or a personality conflict.

Assess the person's background:

- race, culture, upbringing
- socioeconomic status
- morals, religion and values including sexual values
- pre-morbid personality, home behaviour (ask the family).

If possible seek an opinion about the problem from the person with dementia, or consider that the behaviour might be the only way she or he is able to communicate.

The situation

Look at all the circumstances that might be contributing to this problem. Sometimes it is the most unlikely thing that is the reason for the behaviour.

When and where does the problem happen? Does the person always act in this way in the same place? In similar surroundings? Does it always happen with the same person or in similar circumstances?

Who are the other people involved? Is it staff, visitors, a family member, a friend?

At this point we have a pattern of the problem. We have identified the behaviour that everyone finds a problem. We are clearer about the circumstances that contribute to the problem. We may have found out by now that the behaviour is not the real problem — we have found the core and the trigger for the behaviour. We can now plan a strategy to find a solution.

Planning a strategy

What am I going to do about it? In planning the way we are going to respond to the situation we need to access all the appropriate resources available. If it is possible, include the person with dementia in the planning; he or she may well come up with a solution, as may others with dementia if they are involved.

Person with dementia

Decide how much he or she comprehends. Can using the person's likes and dislikes, habits etc. contribute to the solution?

Family

Look at how family and friends could assist either with information or intervention if the person is in residential care. The home carer and the family are a most valuable resource; they have lived with the person with dementia for a lifetime and may have experienced this problem before. Within the family there may be one member who has a better understanding of the problem and ideas on what can be done about it.

Staff

If in residential care find out if there is one member of staff who has already solved the problem, or one who has the most influence with the resident or who comes from the same cultural background.

Community agency

Check if there is a professional or organisation that can help with the problem. A leisure or religious facility may be able to assist. In residential care cultural factors may be the key. Seek help from an appropriate agency.

Now we are on the way to devising a strategy to find a solution. Following are examples of successful outcomes using the problem solving approach.

Example 1

Philippa (see chapter 4) had a problem with one of the men in her care in the nursing home's dementia section. She believed that he was continually seeking sexual satisfaction, daily visiting women residents throughout the facility. The fact that he had a wife who visited regularly, together with her own values on marital fidelity, further influenced Philippa's attitude towards him and she dwelt on the motivation for his behaviour until she could no longer be civil to him. So incensed was she by his behaviour that she requested management to either transfer him to another section or sedate him so that he was not so inclined to go on 'his female visits'.

Defining the problem

By the time a mediator was consulted the situation had deteriorated and a number of staff were involved. Some supported Philippa's view that the resident was 'a dirty old man', while others said that he was 'harmless'. Working relations became strained. The mediator provisionally redefined the problem as staff conflict because of differing moral attitudes.

Assessing the person in the situation

The mediator called a staff conference and listened to all

viewpoints, talked to the man in question and observed his contact with female residents. She noted that none of the women seemed disturbed when he came to see them, on the contrary they all seemed quite pleased, some reaching out to hold his hand or kiss him on the cheek. She was refused permission by the management committee to contact the family caregiver as it was contrary to the policy of the organisation to involve relatives in resident problems. She was not able to uncover any evidence that the male resident was sexually interested in the women even though Philippa was becoming more adamant that the behaviour was sexual. Staff mood was worsening.

Planning a strategy

The mediator's short-term goal was to negotiate with the management committee for permission to interview a relative. This was eventually granted. Information from the wife led to a further assessment. The man was a Legatee for many years and looked after a number of families in the local district. Many of the veteran's widows he helped were now resident in the nursing home. When the wife visited they would often wander around to talk to these old acquaintances, and she supposed that from habit he would also 'keep doing his rounds'. After an explanation to staff, peace was restored and working relations returned to normal. All were happy except Philippa. She said that she could not accept that a man would want to contact so many women unless he had some ulterior motive.

The problem had become more specific. There was not a resident behaviour problem in the first place, the problem was Philippa's attitude which even with help she was unable to change. Because of her competence as a nurse, she was retained by the organisation in charge of a small all female section and requested to undergo counselling to examine her attitude towards male residents.

In this instance, the mediator not only needed to focus on the behaviour and assess the circumstances contributing to the problem, she also had to deal with what turned out to be the main difficulty — staff conflict which was contributing to a deteriorating quality of care in the facility. While staying focused on the main objective, she also recognised the need to achieve short-term goals, for example permission from the management committee to involve relatives. The importance of cooperation from management when resolving some problem situations is highlighted in this case.

Example 2

> Mr Jackson's aggression had become a problem in the nursing home. At the direction of management he was confined in his room for most of the day. When staff came into his room he hit out at them and threw objects. A fairly new resident, he had been admitted from a major hospital after amputation of his second leg and in a moderately severe stage of Alzheimer's disease. From the time he arrived he would throw off the bed covers and lie with the lower part of his body exposed. This behaviour led the nurse in charge of the section to accuse him of harassing the young girls [female staff] for sex. 'We're not having any of that here.' Transfer to another nursing home was arranged. The accompanying report on transfer to the new facility described him as 'a sexual deviant, indecent exposure, sexual harassment of staff and extreme aggression'. Using the problem solving approach, the new facility carried out a total assessment.
>
> **Defining the problem**
> Initially the problem of sexual deviance and aggression was accepted by the second facility. Mr Jackson had stripped off twice in his first three days there, but there had been no sign of aggression and he had not presented as a problem for staff of the new unit. They agreed that a desirable outcome would be for the behaviour not to recommence and they set this as their

objective. If it did, they would try to find some effective technique of responding.

Assessing the person in the situation
Staff drew the following profile of Mr Jackson using information from the previous facility and from his family, a daughter, who cared for him prior to him being admitted to the previous nursing home:

Mr Jackson is an eighty-six-year-old dementing man who has suffered from diabetes for a number of years and is dependent on oral medication which was administered by staff of the previous nursing home. His blood sugar was tested once daily one hour after lunch, measuring between 1.5 and 3. He is described by the first nursing home as having behaved in 'an indecent way' almost from the time he was admitted and the only way staff felt they could protect other residents and handle his behaviour was to keep his door closed. Anti-depressants were prescribed when he became morose and tearful. A sedative prescribed for this aggression did not seem to decrease his outbursts and for the week or two before he was transferred to the new facility his behaviour had become violent. Daughter says he was diagnosed with Alzheimer's disease about ten years ago and is now unable to converse in an intelligible way but she thinks that sometimes he understands what she says to him. Occasionally at home he threw off the bed covers, but did not object to her covering him up again; daughter thinks he took his pants off because he was hot. A wonderful father and always a gentle sort of a man, she had never known him to be bad tempered. Daughter says he seemed very unhappy when she visited him at the previous nursing home, but staff told her the problem was because of the dementia and his deteriorating behaviour. She suggests that the problem might be with the way the previous nursing home treated him. Also his greatest pleasure is spending time in the garden, something that was not available in the previous nursing home.

A somewhat different picture of Mr Jackson was beginning to emerge.

Strategy

As a trial it was decided to alter Mr Jackson's environment by moving him from a single room to a two-bed room. He was wheeled into the garden twice weekly where he seemed quite content and watched the passing traffic with some interest. After consultation with a geriatrician, sedative dosage was decreased over the next two weeks with no return of aggressive behaviour. Results from a glucose tolerance test indicated a very low blood sugar. Examination also revealed considerable pain in the right stump for which treatment and pain killers were prescribed.

Already the whole complexion of the 'problem behaviour' has changed. Mr Jackson's aggressive behaviour did not reappear, probably because of the combination of changed accommodation arrangements, an activity he enjoyed (the garden) and the caring manner of staff. Treatment for a painful stump would also have made him physically more comfortable.

Monitoring of blood sugar levels revealed that the levels were continuously low and the nurse supervisor noted that at times, when Mr Jackson stripped off, he was sweating profusely and trembling, most probably from hypoglycaemic attacks. Divesting himself of clothes would have relieved his discomfort. She assumed that his more volatile behaviour when staff were present was his way of communicating his distress.

Working on this hypothesis, staff were directed to provide a glass of sweetened orange juice when he had an 'attack' to elevate his blood sugar, quietly reassure him and cover him and/or wheel him out into the garden when the attack subsided. Further medical examination confirmed the nurse's observations; diabetic medication was modified and monitored.

Now the picture of the problem has changed completely. The so-called sexual exposure was an attempt to obtain relief from physical discomfort and the reason for the aggressive outbursts in the first nursing home was probably due to the harsh treatment Mr Jackson received there. The problem underlying the whole undesirable situation was his physical condition. In the first nursing home the nurse supervisor and staff were contributing to the behaviours that they labelled 'challenging and indecent' and subsequently unable to handle.

> Mr Jackson lived a fairly contented life for another year, without sedatives and anti-depressants and with proper attention to his diabetes. He died of a heart attack.

Example 3

The situation with Bruce and his young friend (see page 41) was also satisfactorily resolved using the problem solving approach. You will recall that Bruce confided to the day club supervisor that he had 'assaulted' a young friend and he felt distressed and guilty about it. Bruce agreed to a referral to the social worker at the local Aged Care Assessment Team.

Defining the problem
Bearing in mind that Bruce was her client, the social worker accepted his definition of the problem — that he was distressed and guilty as a result of the incident. He was not only upset by his action but also apprehensive about the way his wife was going to react and the reactions of the girl, Sarah, and her family. It seemed fairly certain that several people had, or would have, a problem too. Bruce commented, 'Nobody will want to have anything to do with me now and I don't know what to do'.

Assessing the person in the situation
The effects of Bruce's dementia rendered him unable to assist in finding a solution, but he agreed with the social worker that his wife was the best person to help him 'straighten out this mess'.

Mrs [Bruce] in discussion together with her husband and the social worker, confided that Sarah's mother had told her about the incident and was calling it sexual assault. Mrs [Bruce] said she was frantic, she knew Bruce wouldn't harm a hair of Sarah's head if he was 'normal'; the two families had been life-long friends and their children had grown up together. 'Sarah is', said Mrs [Bruce] 'like a daughter to Bruce, and now it looks as though what he's done is going to make enemies of us. I don't know what to do, I don't want to hurt him and I don't want to lose my friends'.

So it was established that Mrs [Bruce] also had a problem.

At Mrs [Bruce]'s request the social worker talked to Sarah and her parents, and persuaded them to have a joint interview with Bruce and his wife. That first interview was emotionally charged with a gamut of feelings: guilt, distress, anxiety, shock, anger, rejection and grief for a shattered friendship. Sarah herself not only felt shocked but partly responsible for provoking Bruce's action.

The assessment had now expanded; not only did Bruce and his wife have problems that needed sorting out, but so did Sarah and her parents.

Over three interviews, the social worker:
- encouraged everyone to express his or her feelings about the incident and express an opinion
- supported Bruce in his explanation of the incident
- gave information about the effects of dementia and in particular the brain damage that may have contributed to Bruce losing control
- elicited that all wanted to mend their relationship and asked each one to suggest how this could be done.

The outcome was that all were prepared to resume contact and understood and agreed that there would need to be a healing process. Sarah wanted to resume her visits to Bruce and said that she would be more circumspect about the clothes she wore.

There are two significant factors in this example: the professional acumen of the day club supervisor in referring Bruce to a specialist practitioner and the social worker focusing on Bruce as her client and therefore seeking his agreement before each step and including him in all negotiations. We can only imagine what might have happened if the supervisor had taken no action.

The problem solving approach:

- focuses on the person in a problem situation, rather than the behaviour
- offers another option for dealing with difficult situations
- provides an added skill for professional workers
- avoids terms such as 'managing', 'controlling' or 'challenging'
- talks about
  - problems and problem situations
  - assessing the situation or looking at the circumstances
  - finding a solution
  - responding to the person
- removes the concept of 'blame' from the person with dementia, family and worker
- is the most effective way to deal with situations which involve interpersonal relationships.

CHAPTER
7

The effect of dementia on marriage and families

Note: In this chapter the word marriage is used synonymously with partnership as are the words wife/husband, spouse and partner.

The changes that take place in the personality and behaviour of a person with dementia have a profound effect on a partnership and by extension on all members of a family.* Sexual behaviour that is uncharacteristic for the affected person, or that which is considered to be indecent, can be heartbreaking for partners who often feel at a loss to understand these changes and feel helpless dealing with them. For some it is the 'last straw' in the disintegration of the relationship. Others, where a deep love has built up over the years, will view sexual changes as part and parcel of the general deterioration of the affected person, and will respond in much the same way as they do to other behavioural changes.

---

* Because of the paucity of research material on sexuality and dementia, some of the conclusions drawn are those of the author, based on interviews with and opinions of caregiving partners and adult children.

The nature of sexual relationships

Sexuality cannot be considered in isolation from all the other dimensions that go to make up a close and intimate relationship. The intimate feelings and sexual activity of a couple are entwined with the degree of love and regard they have for each other. In turn that love and regard impact on the amount of satisfaction and fulfilment they obtain from their sexual activity. Before considering the impact that dementia has on individual partnerships, it is necessary to examine the nature of marriage, particularly in relation to older people.

Patterns of relationships

There has been a remarkable change in the pattern of intimate relationships in older people and, while it is possible that this change has been evolving for some time, it is only of late that it has been openly recognised. Previously old people were, or were considered to be, either long-time married, widowed or single, whereas we are now seeing a variety of partnerships. With increasing longevity, marriages are lasting into greater old age. It is also becoming more commonplace for second marriages to take place between people in their sixties and seventies and even in their eighties after they have lost a lifetime partner. There is a growing conviction among old people that it is no longer obligatory to remain in an intolerable domestic situation or in a marriage that is no longer a marriage, and this has led to a higher divorce rate in this age group and a readiness to take another partner. Reflecting a general change in moral attitudes, some old people opt out of marriage when taking a new partner, even though they have a deep commitment to that person. Same gender relationships may endure into old age with the same emotional and practical dynamics as many heterosexual relationships.

A close relationship that is often overlooked is that of two men or two women who, because they do not wish to marry or have been left without a heterosexual partner, have set up house together. This type of relationship has no sexual dimension but often has the same degree and variety of closeness and inter-dependency as any other, and is not uncommon among old people.

Choice of partner

There are many reasons why two people are drawn together and it is said that for many the attraction of one person to another is largely unconscious. One theory suggests that opposites attract, that is we select our life partners in order to provide those features of our own personalities that are deficient. The notion is that the needs, desires and personality traits of one will complement those of the other. For example, people who are self-effacing or cannot bring themselves to be assertive or confrontational may select part-ners who have much more aggressive natures. The person who is highly moral and circumspect may select someone who is unin-hibitedly outspoken or who has a repertoire of sexual stories or lewd jokes. This theory also suggests that in selecting opposites, we indicate those parts of personality that exist within ourselves but that we are unable to express. Conversely someone who needs affirmation of his or her own identity might choose a partner who has a similar personality, needs and desires. This may lead to a marriage where the partners are unlikely to confront issues or each other.

Another theory suggests that we choose partners with the type of personality we are familiar with such as a parent or someone else who has had an influence on our lives, so that the partnership will in many respects reflect earlier relationships. In some circum-stances choice can be at a more conscious level, with the couple considering such things as commonality of background, individual needs and wishes, and respect for each other's differences. What-ever the basis for the way we select our partners, life experiences either encountered in the growing-up years, or in a previous rela-tionship, or both, will determine or at least influence not only the choice of a partner but also the quality and life of the partnership.

Marital roles

The roles that each partner plays in a marriage develop gradually, being explicitly and/or implicitly negotiated by the partners over time. In contrast to modern marriages where roles tend to be blurred, in marriages between people in the past gender was a definitive factor in determining each partner's role. For example, the male partner would be responsible for earning the wage and deciding how the money would be spent, paying the bills and looking after the business dealings of the household, disciplining the children, decision making for the family, making household repairs and mowing the lawn. Female roles were equally prescribed. Fewer wives worked outside the home so that shopping and cooking, sweeping, polishing, dusting, washing, ironing and sewing and looking after children and husbands, was their lot. Of course not all partners kept rigidly to this division of labour but this was the general pattern.

Other less tangible roles emerge during the life of a marriage. One partner may become the peacemaker, while another may take on the role of organiser or nurturer who facilitates a climate where family members can grow as independent human beings, change and adapt to new circumstances, and develop self-esteem. One partner may be the one to depend on, the other dependent. Some couples share these roles as well as a togetherness in establishing the rules they live by – constraints on personal behaviour, the handling of freedom of expression and interchange of emotions, joys, secrets and shame. It is probably these intangible roles that have the most influence on the functional quality of any marital-type relationship.

The life of a partnership

A marriage is a complex relationship. The couple has to come to terms with factors ranging from the intensity of emotional closeness to the implications and consequences of the stresses and strains placed on the partners by outside pressures. These can include such things as financial worries, the upbringing of children, job losses and retirement. It is worth noting the social change that couples who are now old have experienced in their lifetime: the drug culture, permissive sexual behaviour, changes in attitudes towards marriage and the ease of obtaining a divorce.

The change in the status of women has had a significant effect on many older marriages. Many men found it difficult to come to terms with the impact of a wife's new-found independence and freedom, and for some this seriously threatened the concept of their own maleness, integrity and self-esteem. Some could not adapt to the change or modify their roles within the marriage. One man told his story to a men's support group.

> One of her friends asked her to go along to some class or other run by the university — our marriage had always been happy. She was always a very good wife, kept the house and the kids looking top hole and she never did anything I didn't agree with and was a wonderful companion. Anyway I took it as a bit of a joke at first. I knew she didn't have the brains for that sort of thing and I wanted to protect her from making a fool of herself and I told her so. Anyway she did keep going and she changed. She began to argue with me about all sorts of things and wanted me to give her an allowance and it was not as though I ever kept her short of money. When she wanted to buy clothes, I'd always give her what she asked for. She said that I never listened to her. I began to feel as though I didn't matter any more. Another thing — I sort of lost my confidence. One night when she went to class, I locked her out of the house. I felt quite ashamed next morning, and she didn't speak to me for nearly a week after that. Well, that was the beginning of the end. Our marriage went to pieces after that, she had changed so much. Then she went to university and got herself a job and I just didn't know how to handle it. That was over twenty years ago and I've never married again. She wrecked my life with all that nonsense.

A marital relationship is a dynamic system with moment-to-moment interaction between the partners. People seldom grow and develop in the same way or at the same rate, and there is continual need to make personal adjustments to maintain or restore a balance in the relationship. When one partner changes, it affects the other who reacts to the new circumstance by adapting his or her own behaviour or plans to accommodate the change in the partner. All marriages have their peaks and troughs; all marriages experience some degree of disagreement and friction and partners tend to develop patterns of conflict resolution (some functional, some dysfunctional) and patterns of responding to and dealing with life's crises. Effective patterns of communication and interaction between partners where each one considers the needs and desires of the other as well as their own contribute to the success of a marriage. The way that partners deal with the positive and negative aspects of their marriage will greatly influence their sexual desires and their sexual satisfactions.

By the time partners in a marriage reach old age their patterns of interaction and dealing with life's vicissitudes have usually become stable and more or less habitual. They have settled into a relationship which, while not always satisfactory, has reached a point of balance as a result of continuing adaptation to each other and to external factors. Within this context they can function as a couple in a way in which they feel comfortable or at least find tolerable. People who have entered into a relatively new relationship in old age will either bring to the partnership already established interactional patterns that have worked for them in the past or will quickly develop new patterns.

Dementia and partnerships

Serious changes that take place later in life, such as one partner becoming demented, will bring about a major imbalance in a partnership. The dementing partner invariably loses his or her sense of self and the capacity to carry out the partnership roles that have been established. Being unable to carry on a sensible conversation or fully comprehend what is happening around them, together with a fading recognition of the partner, will seriously affect the quality and compatibility of the relationship.

Companionship arrangements formed over the years will gradually be undone. Partners who have shared their interests and leisure activities will have less in common and social activities and friendships may be difficult to maintain because of the behaviour of the affected partner and the unaccepting attitudes of others. This will often lead to social isolation. When companionship arrangements have been based on each partner accepting the other's individual pursuits, the 'well' partner may no longer be able to maintain independent interests because of time taken up in caring.

Because the partner with dementia is no longer able to take part in restoring the balance within the marriage, the other one now has the sole responsibility of restoring some sort of order to the relationship. Inevitably this is done by the 'well' partner learning and implementing an entirely new pattern of marital behaviour. When sex has been a highly valued factor in the partnership a major change in the sexual balance can also place extra strain, not only on the caring partner, but often on the affected person as well. The stories of marriages in this chapter illustrate a number of marital patterns and the impact that dementia has had on these relationships.

A balance restored

Mr and Mrs Cox are in their late fifties and have been married for over thirty years. This is Mrs Cox's experience:

We'd always rubbed along together pretty well in our marriage. Nothing very exciting, but we'd never had a row, hardly an argument really. He did his thing and I did mine. [He], you know, looked after the money and the garden and fixed things and I looked after the house and the cooking — and him of course. Nothing ever upset him, he'd just walk away from it. Never talk about it, so I just learned to live with that. If I was upset I just kept it all locked up inside of me and then when my daughter grew up, I could talk to her. He wasn't a great one for sex, once a week sort of thing, Saturday night — that was about it. I could have done with more. Once I thought I'd have an affair, if I could find someone. As a matter of fact, I thought something was wrong with him — physically that is. When he was about forty he just didn't want it any more at all. He wouldn't go and see about it and it did cross my mind that he might be turning into a homosexual. Well, when he got Alzheimer's disease our nice quiet life changed. Now it's all ups and downs and it's all very hard to put up with. He never stops talking now, just follows me around the house, nagging at me all the time. He just doesn't seem to care about paying the bills any more and we had our light cut off twice last year. The place is going to rack and ruin. I asked him to put a screw in a chair the other night and I found him hammering in a six inch nail. One good thing has come out of it, though, he's been able to get an erection again and he wants sex just about every night. But I can put up with that.

You get the impression that Mr and Mrs Cox had established a pattern of interaction over the thirty years of their marriage that, while as she says 'was nothing very exciting', had nevertheless seemed to have superficially met each other's needs, except of course for her sexual needs. While the balance of the marriage had been destabilised by Mr Cox's inability to fulfil his established roles and by his unfamiliar behaviour, it had been partly restored for Mrs Cox by the fulfilment of her sexual needs.

Change in sexual interest

A major dilemma facing a couple can be a marked change in the sexual appetite of the person with dementia.

Decreased interest

Some 'well' partners seem to accept a decline in sexual interest and activity more easily than others. This appears to be particularly so when there have been other facets of the partnership that have been satisfying, and when there has been consideration of the wishes of the partners with regard to sexual activity. As the dementia advances, the affected person may not be able to sustain even the minimal attention necessary for intercourse or manual stimulation. Under these circumstances, engaging in any sexual activity will be extremely difficult and frustrating for some while others, having for years feigned interest to satisfy a spouse's sexual appetite, will express great relief when sexual desire declines and sexual activity ceases. Of course some people will deeply regret the absence of this important part of their relationship.

Increased demand

A higher demand for sexual gratification can be eminently satisfying for some couples, in some circumstances balancing out the negative aspects that the dementia has brought into the relationship, as in the case of Mrs Cox. On the one hand, some couples who have experienced a rich and rewarding partnership and great enjoyment from making love, report that the depth of their intimate feelings for each other and sexual fulfilment have endured. To some extent the same can apply to the couple for whom sexual activity itself has been the main bonding factor throughout the partnership.

On the other hand, an increased demand for sexual gratification can create difficulties for the carer trying to respond to the intensity of the sexual desire of the partner. This is especially so when the couple's sex life has been over for some time and there is a sudden recurrence of sexual activity. A dementing spouse who is no longer able to be attentive or responsive, but who aggressively demands sex, can dramatically reduce the sexual attraction in the relationship. Cognitive changes may result in loss of concentration and the inability to complete intercourse. The spouse, not wanting to deny the partner's demands for sex, will become resigned to repeated failure. Many carers do their best to accommodate the sexual desires of their partners although there does seem to be a gender difference in the way that male spouses respond to the sexual demands placed upon them. Men seem to employ more manual love-making techniques than women in order to satisfy their partners, as well as taking full advantage of occasional erections. Women seem to have many and more varied problems than men in coping with increased sexual demands although some go out of their way to satisfy a spouse. The frequent comment made by female partners, 'It's only sex now, not making love any more', may be indicative of the emotional response women are said to have about the sexual act.

A change in the 'way it is done', can also be difficult for some women to accept. One wife was horrified when her husband asked to be masturbated to help him reach a climax. Manual stimulation had not been a part of their pattern of sexual arousal and she was at a loss to know how to respond. Another wife, shocked after her husband's vicious sexual onslaught, said that she felt as though she had been raped. (This is discussed in more detail in chapter 10.) For some partners an aggressive and continual demand for sex may prompt them to seek residential care for the dementing partner or act as a justification for them to end a shaky marriage.

Because of a decrease in lubrication and elasticity of the vagina, many older women suffer physical discomfort, even pain on penetration. This is more so when sexual activity is suddenly recommenced after a lapse of some time. Hilda told her story to her medical practitioner.

Her husband Trevor had suddenly become interested in sex again after ten years. He was so assertive in his demands that he was wanting sex several times a day and again during the night. Even though he would be satisfied each time, it seemed as though he immediately forgot and would ask her again, sometimes only half an hour later. She said, 'It seems as though the Alzheimer's has driven everything else out of his mind these days'. His erections were frequent even though they only lasted a short time. It had become so painful that she would avoid him as much as she possibly could while still caring for him. She said that even though she still loved him, she was reluctant to kiss him or hug him, as she had been in the habit of doing, because she was frightened it might stimulate his desire for sex.

Frustration and resentment, as well as anger and impatience, can be the lot of both partners when sex is unsatisfying. The partner with dementia may experience deep feelings of rejection and abandonment if their needs cannot be met. A wife in the video, 'A thousand tomorrows', relates how when she could not respond to her husband's request for sex one day, he asked her, 'If you can't do it, will you find me someone who can?'

When the partner is forgotten

A major hindrance to satisfying sex or even to tolerable intimate activity for the well partner, is the common circumstance of no recognition of the life partner by the dementing person. Nor is there any comprehension as to where the spouse fits into the life of the person with dementia. Mrs Morse's story is representative of the experience of many wives, and variously of some male partners:

> The other day he asked me for sex and he even kept an erection until I came. He hasn't been able to do that for, it must be over a year. But when we had finished and I was cuddling him, he told me that I'd better go before his wife came home, because she would be very angry if she found me in bed with him. Well I've heard that sometimes men forget their wives when their mind goes, but when it happens it's an awful shock — and him having passionate sex with someone he thought was a stranger too! Me, his wife! I kept telling him that I was his wife, but he just kept saying no, no. I'd read somewhere that if I went outside and came back again he would remember me and that's what I did, and that worked. But what's making it worse is that I've been remembering that before he got this thing, he was a real charmer — a real ladies' man — and I began to wonder if he had been having affairs with other women all of our married life and been clever in hiding it from me. Ever since that night I've been going over and over things that happened, you know — times when he worked back or had to go on trips interstate. It's been preying on my mind — can't sleep for thinking about it. But then

I really didn't have any reason to doubt him and my children say that there was no way he would have been unfaithful to me. Still I wonder, I can't help it.

Shortly after this Mrs Morse asked for her husband to be transferred to a dementia-specific unit. During the assessment she told the psychologist that she was devastated that her husband no longer knew her, but could still be passionately sexual with her.

A somewhat different experience was that of Mr James's wife who had been separated from him for several years.

When he became afflicted with Alzheimer's disease, she brought him back to the family home to look after him, setting him up with his own room and bathroom. This appeared to work out fairly well for some time, but it seemed that the period they had been separated and the reasons why were gradually being erased from his memory. He began to relate to her in the way he had when they were together and one night she found him wandering in her bedroom. A week or two later she woke to find him lying on her bed, his desire for sex unmistakable. Later on during her visits to him in the nursing home, Mr James obviously had no memory of their separation and from time to time made aggressive sexual overtures.

To have or not to have

For some caring partners, one of the most difficult issues to grapple with is the morality of having sex with someone who may not be fully aware of the nature of their partnership. Often they will feel that they are taking advantage of the person with dementia in order to fulfil their own needs for sexual gratification. Other partners will see the continuation of their sexual life as perfectly normal and appreciate the mutual satisfaction they both derive from making love. This was apparent in a small study of couples (Wright, 1996), which found that sexual intimacy took place twice as often in the Alzheimer's group compared to the control group of 'well' couples.

One client told me that being able to enjoy sex with her dementing partner gave her a feeling that there was still a bond between them. As she said, 'It's all we have left and while we can do it, we jolly well will'.

Husbands in particular will agonise over whether or not they are taking advantage of someone who is no longer able to comprehend the meaning of the marital relationship when they make love to their wives. 'Do you think I'm raping my wife?' is a question that confronts many professionals. Another is, 'Does my wife think that she is a teenager now?' Someone has told him or he has read somewhere that people with dementia go back to a childhood state and he experiences serious doubts about his motivation every time he makes love to her. He can be ambivalent. If his wife has a strong sexual urge, he will respond to her advances but is often unable to complete or enjoy intercourse, becoming overwhelmed with guilt. What has not been explained to him is that even if his wife does have episodes that reflect childhood behaviour or memories, she is not a child and is undoubtedly unaware that she acts this way. There is no need to associate these episodes with the making of a decision as to whether or not to meet her sexual needs. Sometimes the guilt and anxiety a man experiences borders on the extreme and counselling is necessary to ease his anxiety.

Don P. consulted a professional for help because of his extreme anxiety about his sexual relationship with his wife Edith whose Alzheimer's disease was fairly advanced. This is an extract from his story:

> We've just had our fiftieth wedding anniversary, I know it's silly but I still think of her as my beautiful curly-haired girl. We've always been very close but I never thought much about our sex life. Looking back though I realise that we did a lot of cuddling and kissing — and going to bed with her at night was like heaven. You see, we could never have any children so for all those years we were everything to each other. That's just how we were, still are as far as I'm concerned. When I bath her I still love

to touch her body and she seems to really enjoy that, and sometimes she puts my hand on her breast or in other private places and I still get the same feelings that I did when I was a young man. Feel like I'm a teenager again. Well I can't rise to the occasion much any more, but just sometimes I can satisfy her and me too for that matter. We still manage to satisfy each other in other ways — you know what I mean. But the other day I went to a meeting at the hospital for people like me who look after their relatives at home and the woman there said that people with dementia go back to when they were children. And I didn't know what to think. I'm not into assaulting kids. I'm betwixt and between. Feel I can't touch her like that any more and she gets angry with me when I can't, and I know that she is very frustrated. Me too for that matter.

From lover to nurturer

The major shift in roles from wife or husband to carer is another difficult adjustment for the caregiving partner to make. The combination of constant supervision, sometimes bordering on protection; physical care such as bathing, dressing and toiletting for a person with whom you can no longer have a sensible conversation, in itself puts enormous strain on the relationship. And if you add to this the stress of dealing with unfamiliar and sometimes demanding and disruptive behaviour and the inevitable physical and emotional exhaustion of the caring partner, the essence of the relationship is totally changed. In the video, 'A thousand tomorrows', a wife, expressing her sorrow about the deterioration of her sexual relationship with her husband, says 'Sexual intimacy is as much a meeting of minds as of bodies, and when one half of that is gone, then it destroys it all'.

Julie always considered that she and Ted had an ideal marriage. She described them as being 'both very romantic and sexually compatible and making love was a very important part of our marriage'. After Ted had his first stroke he became impotent for some time, but they were still able to have a reasonably satisfying sex life. They talked with each other about how their love-making had altered and promised that whatever happened they would still manage to have sex one way or another. Julie said, 'Of course I never thought that his mind would be affected and I knew I could cope with the bit of paralysis on his right side'. Ted suffered another stroke about a year later and then a few more over the next year or two. Julie said that she noticed that 'his mind began to go — it was as though he wasn't there any more'. When their doctor was consulted, he diagnosed Ted as suffering from a vascular dementia. Julie said that little by little he forgot how to do things and he was 'awfully mixed up'. 'One day', she said, 'he couldn't remember that his shoes went on his feet and eventually it was like looking after a baby — but he didn't forget sex'. She went on, 'Can you imagine making love to someone when you are so tired? At times I wanted to scream at him. It got to the stage where I couldn't sleep in the bed with him any more and I changed it over for two single beds. I'd put him to bed and then wait until he was asleep before I would go. You know it's really impossible to feel romantic when you have to do all those intimate caring things and when you're so exhausted. I do feel rather badly about it as though I have let him down in some way but he doesn't appeal to me in that way any more. I never thought this would happen to us'.

When dementia is associated with a physical disability such as severe paralysis as the result of a stroke or severe tremor as in Parkinson's disease, the impact on romance and intimacy can be sobering. There is often a heavier burden in the care of a partner who is physically disabled and when associated with dementia it can severely inhibit sexual attraction.

When Parkinson's disease is a factor, coping with the tremor and an increasingly 'clumsy' lover can be off-putting, particularly when touching and caressing has been an important part of the couple's sexual pattern.

Bill Jones met Marie at the local Senior Citizens Club a year or two after his wife died. Both in their late sixties, they had been agreeably surprised by the depth of feeling and sexual attraction that developed between them and decided to move into Marie's house and live together. Bill knew that Marie had been diagnosed with Parkinson's disease, but the slight tremor she had in one hand didn't really bother him and he assured her that he would always be there to look after her. Caressing was a very important part of their romantic life; holding hands at odd moments and the stroking and the sensation of closeness of their naked bodies when they made love. But as her tremor worsened, he developed an aversion to her touch, often shuddering and quickly brushing her hand away when she shook and fumbled while trying to stimulate him. Marie became increasingly confused until, as Bill explained, 'it seemed like the two [deterioration of mind and body] met at a peak and I just couldn't handle the shaking and the confusion any more. But the sad part of it is that she still remembers who I am, and she still wants sex'. I still love her, but I can't bring myself to get close to her body any more. But I couldn't feel any more responsible for her if we were married. She can't do anything at all for herself anymore and I'll take care of her till the end'.

Incontinence

The impact of incontinence on sexual activity even though it seems to rarely take place during sexual intercourse, cannot be underestimated. When the affected partner becomes incontinent, it can be the finish of sexual attraction. Some partners say that the image of cleaning and washing the affected partner of urine and sometimes faeces will suddenly penetrate the fantasy and emotion of the sexual act and sex can become abhorrent. In one husband's words, 'It's a passion killer'.

In sickness and health

There are spouses who manage to cope reasonably well with an incontinent partner and do not allow incontinence, or other behaviours, to significantly interfere with their intimate lives. Others feel bound by their marriage vows and affirm total loyalty to those vows – to look after their partners 'in sickness and in health' including looking after their sexual needs. Sometimes spouses will also say that, despite incontinence, there is no way they would move either themselves or their dementing partners out of the marital bed, even though they may have to change the sheets several times during the night. Or they say they would never contemplate rebuffing the partner's sexual advances, even though they no longer get any pleasure from sex, 'Because it is the only pleasure [he] has left in life and I couldn't take that away from [him]'.

Negotiating new patterns

In the early stages of the dementia illness, and where alteration in sexual behaviour is a factor, some couples have been able to renegotiate their patterns of arousal and intimacy when unexpected changes appear. Techniques such as intimate touching, massaging and mutual masturbation substitute for penetrative intercourse. When new patterns can be established sufficiently early in the course of the dementia, they appear to be maintained for some time into the later stages.

Effects of residential care

When the person with dementia is transferred from home into residential care, not only does he or she have to make significant adaption to the separation and a new routine, but so does the partner. A carer wife or husband will have to come to terms with a loss of personal identity in that they are stripped of familiar marital roles and of the bond with a life partner who may no longer recognise them as such. Partners invariably have mixed feelings: relief, sadness, guilt and loneliness and many will experience difficulty in coming to terms with the perception, sometimes erroneously, that they are now superfluous to their spouse's care and life. They may find it hard to accept another person, particularly of the opposite sex, performing intimate caring tasks for the dementing partner, even though they may appreciate the common sense of this arrangement. One woman complained:

> When the nurse came in with a bottle, she asked me to leave the room. How do you like that? I'd been married to him for fifty years and looked after him when he was sick. Who did she think had washed him and cleaned his bottom for the past eighteen months?

Another said:

> I was rubbing his penis — he was always hungry for sex when I came to see him — and this therapist came in and told me to stop it, it wasn't nice. Well I told her that I paid for this room and what went on between me and my husband was none of her business.

And another:

> It's a good nursing home. I always feel welcome and I think they're glad of the help on the days that I shower and dress him and feed him. He shares a room with another man, but when I visit, they make sure that we can use the room by ourselves. Then if we want to do a bit of smooching, I know nobody is going to interrupt us.

Influence of family and friends

Family members and friends can be of considerable support to the caregiving partner, particularly in a time of major crisis such as a shift from home to nursing home or special care hostel. With a sympathetic ear they can help the relinquishing spouse come to terms with the complex emotional trauma associated with nursing home admission and the complications of the unhealed hurts and the recriminations, 'if only ...' and 'I wish I had ...' or 'I wish I hadn't ...'

The spouse also needs time and freedom to work through the maze of feelings that are associated with 'losing' a partner with whom there is still an emotional tie, and sometimes the vision of a bleak and sterile future. In circumstances where the separation is not so traumatic, space is still needed for the spouse to reorganise his or her life. This does not always happen. Comments such as 'Why don't you forget about him and leave the nursing home to look after him' do not help. Family and friends offering gratuitous advice will often increase the stress being experienced even when they have the best interests of the 'well' partner at heart.

Rita and Joe emigrated from Italy forty years ago; married in Australia and raised a family of five children (the youngest now twenty-five and the eldest thirty-seven) and established a small and profitable fruit market. They were rarely apart, sharing both the work of the business and bringing up a family. Joe looked after Rita at home for four years after she was diagnosed with Alzheimer's disease until the dementia became so severe that she needed nursing home care. She no longer recognised any of the family, was incontinent, could not feed herself and needed total care. Joe visited her daily, each day becoming more and more upset and depressed. His children tried to persuade him to find himself another lady: 'Mumma doesn't know anything any more'; 'You aren't going to do her any good by crying all the time'; 'Daddy, you're only sixty-three, you have lots of life in front of you, why don't you go out more — meet new people'; 'You've worked hard all of your life dad, enjoy yourself'; 'You don't need to go there [to the nursing home] every day. Mumma won't know if you're there or not. And anyway she'd want you to be happy'. While Joe appreciated the fact that his children cared about him, and he said that he could see the common sense in what they were saying, he felt that by enjoying his life he was in some way being unfaithful to Rita and, if he found another companion, a sinner in the eyes of his church. He was being 'pulled two ways' he said and was in a state of indecision about his life, although the thought of another relationship was not on his agenda. Then one day, he blurted it all out to the carers' group he attended every month and was surprised to find that there were others there who were in the same situation and was overcome with the amount of support that he received. He became friendly with one of the women, recently widowed, and some time after Rita died, they married.

Not all relatives are so supportive, particularly when there are split loyalties within the family, for example with children who were more closely aligned with the parent with dementia when growing up than with the caring parent or when the parent's illness has swayed their affections. Within the family there may be divisions that will make life difficult for the relinquishing partner, particularly if the marriage was generally not satisfactory. While some children will support the 'well' parent, others may resent his or her overwhelming relief that the other parent has gone. Negative feelings that might have been built up over the years may be visited on the 'well' father or mother when the affected parent is admitted to residential care. 'You should have kept on looking after her/him at home. Why don't you visit him/her more often?' When the parent forms a new liaison, the accusations can become more strident. 'You only put him in a home to get rid of him. You've been having an affair behind his back all this time, how could you?', totally overlooking the right of parents to a life of their own, and to live that life as they wish.

Effect on adult children

The effect that a change in sexual behaviour has on family members other than the spouse is often overlooked. Where a daughter is caring for a parent, coming to terms with a change in role from child to 'mother' is in itself a difficult adjustment to make, particularly when a male parent requires intimate care. On occasions when the male parent makes sexual advances to the daughter her reaction is invariably one of horror and disgust, often resulting in a fracturing of the image she carries of her parent and shattering a lifetime relationship. The degree of distress and devastation that some grown children experience has a profound effect on their lives generally, at times necessitating psychotherapy. Sons can also have similar experiences when caring for their mothers, but this situation either does not appear to be so common, or else they are more reluctant to talk about it.

Even more difficult to come to terms with is if a person with dementia (usually male) makes sexual advances to young members, sometimes grandchildren. While this appears to happen only rarely the consequence is usually admission to a residential facility as soon as it can be arranged. Behaviour that is considered to be indecent can have disastrous results both for the family members and the person with dementia.

> Mr Duncan contracted Pick's disease in his fifty-fourth year and was cared for at home by his wife and young adult daughters. A married son and his family were regular visitors. The family had always thought of themselves as being 'close' and Mr Duncan received considerable support from his wife and two daughters in the early stage of the disease. This was until he began to invite his daughters into his bedroom and show them pictures and magazines that they considered to be pornographic. Mr Duncan had always been a highly conservative and moral man, and sex was a subject that had never been discussed openly in the family. The three women would not accept the explanation that he was unaware of his actions or that he might in his muddled way be involving his daughters in some belated sex education. So stunned were they by his behaviour that they didn't want to hear about it, and when they spoke about him, the word incest was often mentioned. Mrs Duncan would no longer allow him to embrace or be alone with his grandchildren. Mr Duncan was admitted to a dementia-specific unit at the request of his wife.

Counselling

When the sexual behaviour of a partner or a parent is causing ongoing distress, it can be helpful to seek counselling from a professional therapist. The therapist should be carefully selected. When help is needed with changes in sexual practices between the partners then the assistance of a sex therapist is indicated. If it is to do with the broader relationship between partners or troubled interaction within the family, then a relationship therapist is required. Either way, the therapist chosen must be an accredited professional with a sound knowledge of dementia and its effect on behaviour, appropriate responses to that behaviour and an appreciation of the modifications that can reasonably be anticipated. An appropriate place to start seeking such help is through a memory disorders clinic, psycho-geriatrician, the treating medical practitioner, hospital social work department or the area Aged Care Assessment Team.

Carers' groups can be good places to share troubles about sexual problems but many group leaders report some difficulty in getting the subject off the ground. It seems that the introduction of the topic of sexuality invariably brings forth a self-conscious reaction from the members, often evidenced by restrained laughter followed by an embarrassed silence. This reaction should be considered as a normal part of the process, the beginning point of the discussion. It is fairly easily overcome by the leader of the group recognising with the members that this can be a difficult subject to talk about. If no one is forthcoming in sharing a personal experience, it is a good idea for the group leader to fill the breach with a previously prepared topic on sexuality which is commonly experienced in intimate relationships.

8

Sexuality and residential care

'The giving and receiving of affection, being valued, having a "safe place" to share and relive memories and to feel unconditional regard, begins at birth and continues throughout the life span.'

(Hoffman & Kaplan, 1996)

Old people who live in the community, including those with dementia, often have opportunities to indulge their sexual desire or channel their unused sexual energy into other activities. In a nursing home or hostel, or when someone lives alone and is socially isolated these opportunities are limited. In most residential facilities they are invariably cut off from the moment-to-moment closeness or the love-making that may have been previously enjoyed. In most care facilities sensuality and sexual desires are more often than not ignored or denied expression. Even mentally alert elderly people in nursing homes may be reluctant or embarrassed to express their feelings about loss of intimacy and sexual satisfaction, and their frustrations may be disguised by a range of emotions and behaviours, from acting out against staff to non-cooperation and depression. This is even more so for the person with dementia whose only means of communication is increasingly through the feelings they display and the way they behave. Deprived of the companionship, affection and at times sexual satisfaction with their life partner and frustrated by an institution's denial of their sexual needs, they may act out their discontentment in a number of ways.

While it is true that some people with dementia reject all affectionate overtures, for others the capacity for intimate contact, warmth, affection and sexual pleasure remain – in some instances in greater strength than before. When a person's mind and behaviour is altered by dementia and normal faculties diminish, sexual desire and need for affection may still exist well after these capacities have declined. When this is so, it is important for the well-being of the person that these needs are in some way fulfilled and careworkers need to be sensitive to the emotions and behaviours that indicate such desires.

> Staff noticed that when Mrs Radcliffe returned from her weekly visits home, she was morose and often tearful for a day or two. When this worsened over time they reduced her weekends at home to once a month. When she still seemed distressed on her return the supervisor of the special hostel, suspecting some form of abuse, confronted Mr Radcliffe. He explained that they had always had a very satisfactory sexual relationship and both still enjoyed this part of their marriage. Shocked at the supervisor's accusation, he complained that on his daily visits to his wife he could only sit with her in a room with a number of other residents with no outlet to demonstrate their affection. Therefore all of their needs for sexual gratification had to be fulfilled on that one weekend. In light of this, it seemed that Mrs Radcliffe's distress might have been the result of the withdrawal of the intimacy she shared with her husband on weekends. Weekly home visits were recommenced and when space was provided in the hostel for them to have private moments together some normality returned to their relationship.

Given that Mrs Radcliffe's distress always occurred in the same circumstances, when she returned from her weekend visits, it is understandable that staff jumped to a wrong conclusion. While they were quick to form the opinion that sexual abuse might be a factor on her visits home, they had completely overlooked the fact that she still experienced sexual needs and desired an intimate relationship with her husband. The opinions of staff in this incident also reflect the tendency to ignore the fact that women have sexual needs. Is this because the sexual desires of women are less likely than men's to be expressed in ways that are more likely to cause a fuss?

Meeting needs in residential care

When a partner is still involved with the resident, and the need for sexual gratification is a factor, it should be a simple matter to provide opportunities and quiet places for the couple to embrace in private and have intimate times together. Another option is for the resident to have regular visits to his or her own home, providing that the partner can cope and that the change of scene does not have any seriously adverse effects on a person with dementia. Sexual relationships between partners are normal and must be regarded as commonplace as any other contact between them, with no embarrassed smirking or mocking from staff.

> The Masons are in their seventies. Up to the time Mr Mason was admitted to the nursing home, they enjoyed a satisfactory sex life. Then he shared a room with three others and when Mrs Mason visited they walked together or sat beside his bed. Visitors were embarrassed when they came upon them in a passionate embrace. Moving Mr Mason into a single room gave them opportunities to be together undisturbed. Both were noticeably less stressed and his advances to female staff became rare.

The security of familiarity

Even when partners are not as close as they used to be, when one is accepted into residential care the need for support from the other can be greater than before. More often than not when a person is moved to a nursing home or special care hostel, he or she will need the emotional security and safety that comes from intimate contact with a person who is familiar in their lives. By not encouraging or ignoring this, we can add to the anxiety caused by the separation from home and family and increase the person's sense of loss of all that is important and familiar.

Remember the last time there was a major change in your life? Did you wonder what the new people in your life would be like? Did you have to find your way around a new location – bus stop, timetables, shops and so on? Maybe you lost your job or you experienced a broken marriage and had to give up your home. Did you have to adapt to a different life role? Were you uncertain about the future? Did you feel helpless? Were you overcome with anxiety or felt insecure until you adjusted to the new situation? In times like these, we usually cling to the person in our lives who is closest to us; the people we can count on for support. We need to depend on them to get us through the crisis, and this may take several weeks or even months. Yet when someone is transferred from home to residential care or into a new situation in that place, such as a move from hostel to nursing home, we often expect the person to adjust to new circumstances in a very short time. Sometimes very little thought is given to the trauma involved.

It is essential to recognise and respond to the anxiety that results from changes and to appreciate the degree of loss and grief associated with a change in location and lifestyle. The new resident has not only to adapt to an unfamiliar environment among a number of strange people but is probably also coming to terms with the reason, often a life-threatening illness or dementia, for seeking residential or nursing home care. New residents suffer multiple losses – familiar sights and sounds and smells and many of the personal contacts and roles in life they hitherto enjoyed. Most of all they have suffered a loss of identity and self-esteem.

Mr and Mrs Smith had a fairly contented and independent life until Mr Smith suffered a stroke. After treatment and rehabilitation he was moved into the nursing home section of the retirement complex where they lived. Even though the hostel where Mrs Smith still lived was only a long corridor away, the organisation of the nursing home made it impossible for them to spend much time together, even less than when he was in hospital. Daily routine of the different sections did not allow for them to take meals together. Staff were reluctant to allow them privacy on the grounds that intimacy and overt affection were not considered appropriate in that nursing home. When he was well enough to leave his room, Mrs Smith was refused permission to wheel him into the garden, let alone take him to their daughter's home for a weekend visit as they had always done. Mr Smith was agitated, constantly asking for his wife, and soon became depressed. Mrs Smith, angry, confided in a counsellor, 'I feel totally depersonalised. After being married to him for over fifty years, I don't seem to count as a wife any more'.

A new director of nursing was appointed. She arranged for Mrs Smith to spend as much time as possible with her husband and encouraged both of them to take some control in planning for his care and recreation. When he was mobile Mr Smith returned to live in their hostel unit.

The need for security

The impact of moving into a residential facility on a person who is affected by dementia is likely to be overlooked. Careworkers believe that because of poor memory and other cognitive defects the person will not be fully aware of the change. But the feeling of being abandoned on changing from one environment to another can be more severe for the person with dementia because of heightened confusion. Sometimes a close relationship is formed with another resident and the reason, or part of the reason, may very well be that the person has been deprived of intimate contact with a life partner. Change may even be more traumatic than for the person who fully understands what is happening. The consequence can be extreme anxiety exacerbated by the person's inability to clearly communicate those feelings. Catastrophic reactions that are triggered by change and not sensitively handled are commonplace.

Opportunities for spending as much quality time as possible with a normal life partner will greatly enhance the ability for residents to adapt emotionally to new or changed circumstances. Even those with dementia will generally make it clear either in words or actions if or when they no longer wish to, or are no longer able to, maintain a close relationship.

Dictating morality

When someone comes into the care of a residential facility, the way that sexuality is considered, if at all, very much depends on the values and policy of the organisation, attitudes of administration and individual members of staff. No one would argue that service providers have a duty of care to protect residents from sexual harm and that this responsibility should not be taken lightly. But there are some places where the administration or the staff, or both, believe that part of this duty of care is a personal responsibility to dictate the morals of the people in their care. Control, however, is often not in terms of the resident's values, rather it is in accordance with the ideology and attitudes of the service providers.

What can happen when attempts are made to control the morality of residents is that someone might be disadvantaged, or even punished for what is considered unacceptable sexual behaviour by the facility. It is still a practice in some facilities where behaviour is interpreted as sexual, for the perpetrator to be so sedated that she or he has little life at all. When someone with dementia cannot comprehend the reason for a careworker's action or why it is that they disapprove, or even why one careworker reacts in a different or even opposite way to another careworker, that person is invariably confused and distressed. The careworker too is sometimes left uncomfortable and vaguely guilty wondering whether a situation might have been much better handled. Under these circumstances, if the values of the resident or the resident's family do not coincide with that of the facility, difficulties are likely to arise and more problems created than there are solved.

Liaisons between strangers Probably the most difficult of situations to handle in residential care are liaisons between people who were strangers before they came to live in a nursing home or hostel. When a person with dementia lives at home with a partner there is usually only one opportunity for a sexual relationship and interactions with others that have sexual overtones are fairly limited. But all this can change when the person with dementia goes into a nursing home or a hostel. With a number of people of both genders living in close physical and social proximity to each other and to staff, sex and sensuality then take on an entirely different complexion. A dementing person may reach out to a member of staff for affection or to another resident for social and personal contact.

One of the most common interactions between two residents is the development of an emotional and physical closeness, often to the exclusion of other residents, staff and family. The memory of any partner has often been obliterated or, if there is recognition of the partner, the nature of the relationship is often forgotten. This is graphically illustrated in the video 'A thousand tomorrows' when a wife, suspecting that her husband no longer knows her asks, 'Do you know who I am?' and he answers that she is one of the people who take care of him. She says, 'I'm your wife!' to which he replies, 'Oh well you might be, but you're not my only wife'.

Attitudinal differences Differences in attitudes will take on a special significance when extra-marital liaisons or those considered to be of an 'illicit' nature are involved. The cocktail of values and feelings of staff mixed with the attitudes and needs of the real-life partner, other family members and the needs and wishes of the person with dementia will inevitably create some difficulties when it comes to untangling the threads of such a relationship. A number of obstacles will invariably have to be surmounted before a solution is arrived at that goes some way towards meeting the approval of all the parties concerned.

Attitudes of professional carers

The quality of the response to sexual and intimacy needs in residential care is greatly determined by staff who can have a profound effect on the life of the resident and on the lives of the partners and families. Residential careworkers who are comparative strangers to a resident have the power to influence and control the moment-to-moment life of a resident and it is the values that are held by careworkers that mostly determine how the behaviour of a resident is judged and, to a lesser extent, how families are treated. In a facility where practices are task-oriented rather than person-focused little consideration will be given to the needs and wishes of the resident or the family. What is considered to be sound management by the facility, may not necessarily be in the best interests of those using the facility.

Where staff attitudes are at odds with organisational policy in matters of resident behaviour – a state of affairs which is commonly experienced – this in itself creates conflict. Some younger staff may have more tolerance of sexual behaviour than older staff, while others are conservative and inflexible when it comes to the behaviour of old people. Feelings of 'like' and 'dislike', either of the resident, partner or family, will more often than not prejudice the way that staff respond to any situation particularly in circumstances where sexuality is concerned.

Given these inconsistencies, attitudes about sexual activity and old people generally, and in particular those in care – 'not right', 'perfectly normal', 'indecent', 'past it', 'sinful', 'depends on the circumstances', 'adulterous', 'darling', 'cute', 'wonderful', 'sweet' – it is not hard to imagine that close liaisons are viewed and treated in so many different ways.* Those who believe that an old person should not have a sexual life will condemn even those people who have no real-life partner living or involved. Others who believe that all people have the right to follow their desires will defend the rights of the people in their care to have their sexual needs fulfilled. These sorts of attitudinal conflicts occur more frequently in residential care, but will also happen from time to time when a person with dementia is being cared for in the community.

> The community nurse was approached on her weekly visit by Mrs Baxter's neighbours who expressed concern that her ex-husband had been 'hanging around' and had been seen the day before trying to climb through the window. Mrs Baxter was unable to give a rational explanation, but had a couple of bruises on one of her arms and seemed distressed when the nurse questioned her. When the daughter's opinion was sought, she reported the nurse to the community team leader complaining of the nurse's inference that her father might be sexually harassing her mother. The team leader transferred the nurse into another area, accusing her of having a 'dirty mind'. Phrases like 'shocked at you', 'invading people's privacy' and 'unprofessional and perverted' were used leaving the nurse in no doubt that the team leader believed that such behaviour was not possible because 'they are past it'. A few weeks later Mrs Baxter was moved to the local nursing home. After a series of incidents, there was no doubt that the ex-husband was forcing his attentions on her. When they insisted that his visits take place in the public lounge room, he did not come any more.

The attitude of the community team leader in this case certainly contributed to the disadvantage of someone for whose well-being she was ultimately responsible. Had her attitude been more flexible about the sexuality of people in the team's care, or had she

* Opinions from professional workers about illicit relationships of people with dementia were given at seminars on aged care conducted all over Australia during 1996.

listened more carefully to the nurse's concerns, Mrs Baxter would have been saved from weeks of abuse.

Attitudes of partners

The way that a partner reacts towards an extra-marital contact is bound up in the relationship with the dementing person. 'Well' partners, even those who are relieved to be free from the emotional and physical exhaustion of caring, may still be grappling with feelings associated with losing control and handing over care to people who are relative strangers. There may be feelings of guilt. There is a gap in their lives, an emptiness, and however illogical it may seem, they can feel abandoned by the partner with dementia. While most partners accept the inevitability of the person's condition, some feeling of grief is usually experienced. There can be disbelief at how far the dementia has progressed and anger (which may be manifested in blaming and questioning, often in association with the quality of care) as well as feelings of sadness and depression at the loss of the person they once knew. A carer's belief that she or he has failed is often prompted or exacerbated by the knowledge that careworkers have the ability to look after their relative when they are unable to do so. Inevitably then, there is a mixture of emotions which influence the way spouses regard liaisons between their partner and another resident, ranging from degrees of acceptance to feelings of being rejected and betrayed. A spouse may, for example, accept a hand-holding relationship between the partner and another resident, but strongly resent it if they are observed lying on a bed together. There are occasions when a partner becomes jealous of the care relationship which springs up between the resident and a careworker, even to the point of regarding the closeness of the professional carer as the final wedge in the marriage.

When we talk about a husband or wife in the area of dementia care, the popular image is of a married couple who have spent a large part of their lives together, and a devoted and often self-sacrificing 'well' partner who is the family carer. Carers' organisa-

tions and the literature tend to reinforce this image and professional workers often have an expectation that carers will fit into
this mould. Of course many do but some do not. When a marriage
is splintered or breaks down, the 'well' partner can be relieved to
be rid of the pressure of trying to maintain a semblance of caring
and support. A new relationship can be the way out of an intolerable situation and provides a reason for visits to the institutionalised partner to cease (although guilt can be experienced when
this happens too).

Professional careworkers come into contact with a variety of
partnerships: marriages both intact and fragmented, cohabiting
couples and second marriages, and partnerships of short duration.
Recognition of gay and lesbian relationships is now more commonplace and service providers are increasingly being faced with
the need to consider the needs and wishes of a number of different
partner combinations. But whatever the nature of the partnership,
when the person with dementia forms a new liaison in a residential facility, there is bound to be a complex and tangled web of
interaction. It must always be remembered, however, that the life
partner is still an integral part of the resident's life, and must be
treated as such, until she or he indicates otherwise.

Attitudes of family members

Some adult children may accept a new relationship of a parent
without question. Others may have strong feelings about what they
consider to be an illicit relationship, and can be embarrassed,
shocked, angry, or all three. It is not unusual for an adult son or
daughter to judge the relationship as unfaithfulness to the other
parent, even though that parent may no longer be living. For some
adult children such a relationship sullies the father or mother image
that has been built up throughout the children's growing years and
this brings with it its own grief. The fact that the parent suffers
from dementia, and is known to be oblivious to the nature of the
relationship, does not seem to soften the hurt.

In some families there is a cultural expectation that one

member, usually a daughter, will accept ongoing responsibility for the care of a parent. This may in itself cause a disagreement in a family if that member is no longer able or willing to meet that responsibility and the parent has to be placed in a residential facility. If the parent forms a relationship in residential care, the family carer often has to bear the blame, sometimes being accused by others, usually siblings, of neglecting the parent and so failing in her duty. Residential care staff may find themselves embroiled in the reverberations of such a family conflict. When a problem situation involves a culture which is unfamiliar to the careworker, consultation with a professional from that culture or the appropriate cultural agency should be sought.

Successful outcomes

The stories that follow are of situations involving relationship dilemmas that were experienced by professional careworkers and how those situations were handled.

Situation 1

Rex Williams had been a resident in the dementia unit for twelve months. When Hetty Jones arrived Rex greeted her like an old friend even though he had not previously known her. They became inseparable, walking around the unit holding hands, sitting together at meals, in the recreation room and on the bus on weekly excursions. When separated they were excessively agitated, pacing the corridors and knocking on doors, until they found each other. Some staff called them 'the lovers', but others were apprehensive about the closeness of the relationship and, when they began to visit each other's rooms, sit on the bed and hug and cuddle, many of the staff were anxious that their behaviour might become overtly sexual. The manager of the unit met with staff and they all agreed that Mrs Williams should be told about Rex and Hetty in order to gauge her reaction. Hetty's husband was dead and she did not have a family. Mrs Williams explained that Rex had always had a great capacity and need for love and affection and had probably missed the moment-to-moment loving that he received at home. She told them that he was not aware of the illicit nature of his relationship with Hetty and that he had not recognised her as his wife for a long long time. She thought of him as a precious dependent child. She was quite agreeable for the relationship to continue and assured staff that they should not worry.

Situation 2

About two weeks after eighty-six-year-old Mrs Smith came to the dementia unit, the personal care assistant knocked on the door prior to helping her to shower. Not receiving an answer, she went in and peeked around the shower door. 'You could have knocked me over with a feather', she told the others afterwards, 'there was that old guy who moved in to the hostel nest door a few days ago. The two of them were stark naked in the shower and he was washing her back. The first thing I thought of was to yell at him to get out, but then I thought better of it. So I just quietly handed them towels and asked them both to come and sit down. Was he embarrassed! He just broke down but she didn't seem to be a bit worried. But I was pretty pleased at the way I handled it'.

The personal care assistant reported the incident to her supervisor. Not wanting to further distress the man, who by this time was fearful of being asked to leave the hostel, the supervisor suggested to him that they talk to Mrs Smith's son. The son explained that the two had been friends for some years, and when his mother needed help because of her Alzheimer's, the friend had moved in to care for her, which he had done conscientiously for two years. When they couldn't cope any more with the household chores and Mrs Smith's advancing dementia, the three of them had decided on residential care. The friend had moved into the hostel to be near her. After several short trial runs, Mrs Smith and her friend were transferred to a double unit where they managed reasonably well with help from a personal care assistant.

Situation 3

The following is a situation of considerable complexity that involved a number of people, but it was diffused with such understanding, sensitivity and love that it needs to be told. So that the reader does not get lost in the maze, the people involved are listed as if they are characters in a play.

Characters

Mr and Mrs Charles — long-time residents in a nursing home
Mr Brian — recent resident in a dementia-specific unit
Mrs Lucy — resident in a dementia-specific unit
Mrs Brian — lives at home
Mrs Mackay — daughter of Mrs Lucy
Staff of dementia-specific unit

Mr and Mrs Charles were in their late eighties and had been married for over sixty years. They lived in a double room in a nursing home for five years until Mrs Charles began to wander. It was decided that she was in need of the special care that was available in the dementia unit attached to the nursing home. Mr Charles was visibly upset by the separation, spending most of his time with her in the dementia unit. One week after she was transferred he died.

Just a day or two later, Mr Brian came to the dementia unit. His likeness to Mr Charles was uncanny — tall, broad and bearded. Mrs Charles greeted him with a kiss and a hug in just the same way as she responded to her husband. She was happier and her pacing and tracking to the door and calling out for her husband ceased. On the occasions that their paths crossed Mr Brian accepted her attentions with obvious pleasure and hand-holding became the order of the day. Every so often they engaged in a bit of plant-pulling in the summer garden and carried on long conversations — heads together on the garden seat — which were unintelligible to anyone else, but of great depth and meaning to them.

For no particular reason Mr Brian was relocated to a room next door to Mrs Lucy, sweet-natured and gentle, pining for her past success as an actress. It was as though the discovery of Mr Brian brought some purpose into Mrs Lucy's desolation. She adopted him as her very own and set about 'caring' for him: introducing him variously as 'my husband', 'my son', 'my friend', feeding him at mealtimes, popping in and out of his room, smoothing the covers on his bed, hugging and stroking him, shepherding him around the unit, never more than a few paces from his side.

Pandemonium reigned! Every time Mrs Charles saw the two together she screamed and spat, often hitting out when they came within reach, one time pulling Mr Brian out of Mrs Lucy's grasp, and shoving him until he lost his balance and fell. At breakfast one day she poured cornflakes and milk over the two of them. In the meantime Mr Brian and Mrs Lucy became closer and closer and Mrs Charles became more and more aggressive.

And what of the staff? They did a wonderful job keeping the combatants apart, mainly distracting Mrs Charles and giving her more than usual attention and affection, and diverting the two sides into different occupations. Mrs Brian, although her husband no longer recognised her as his wife, visited each day and must have been aware of the friendship between her husband and Mrs Lucy but did not bring the matter up with staff. Finally, it was decided that the time had come to involve both Mrs Brian and Mrs Lucy's daughter, Mrs Mackay.

After several meetings during which Mrs Mackay at first reluctantly agreed to the relationship continuing, and Mrs Brian had no objection at all, a plan was devised. Mrs Brian started visiting all three, spending her mornings walking, watching television, 'playing cards' or just sitting and 'chatting'. As there was no overt affection during these visits, largely due to Mrs Brian's intervention, there was also no aggressive backlash. During her twice weekly visits, Mrs Mackay took her mother out of the unit, so removing one of the 'irritants'. The recreation worker devised a program of activities which included the company of a companion for all of them. From time to time staff still needed to distract either one or the other if war appeared likely. There was still the occasional outburst from Mrs Charles but the volatility of the situation was defused undoubtedly due to the changed lifestyle and assisted by the worsening of Mrs Charles's dementia.

An unfortunate outcome

Not all liaisons have such positive outcomes as the above three. The following situation was disastrous for everybody and illustrates the folly of overlooking the extent and seriousness of a problem combined with a lack of communication between those involved. The consequences of a laissez-faire attitude plus deception can mean distress for many people: conflict among staff, disagreement between family and facility and threats of litigation.

Mr Shepherd's daughter accompanied by her solicitor, sought the advice of a private counsellor. Several weeks before when visiting his wife in the nursing home, Mr Shepherd had noticed that a male resident seemed always to be by her side. Staff denied any impropriety, saying that this man liked the company of all the female residents, not only Mr Shepherd's wife. As well, staff went to a great deal of trouble to reassure the adult children that they were not seeing what they thought they were seeing. Not satisfied, Mr Shepherd began to pop in at odd times during the day and evening when he usually found his wife in the close company of the same man. Then one day he came upon them lying on her bed together.

Very angry, Mr Shepherd accused staff of not protecting his wife from sexual harassment and of deliberately deceiving him. One of the nurses explained the influence of dementia on behaviour, but it seemed as though his anger prevented him from fully comprehending what she was telling him. He was determined to take some action and that is how the solicitor came to be involved.

On discussing the matter with staff of the facility the consultant pieced together the following:

Mrs Shepherd and Mr X had become 'friends' almost from the first day they met. Some staff ignored the blossoming of intimacy while others separated the couple at every opportunity. On several occasions they were removed from each other, with Mr X at one stage being transferred to another wing. When apart both became aggressive, at times hitting out and swearing at staff and other residents. Mrs Shepherd spent most of her waking hours pacing and wandering, once running across the road into the bush and being lost for hours. Mr X became uncooperative, refusing to shower and eat. They were reunited for the sake of peace in the unit and very quickly settled.

Early on some of the staff agreed on a plan to handle the matter and they began a deception and 'cover-up'. The couple, they agreed, would simply be separated before Mr Shepherd's usual visiting times and they would deny the existence of the relationship when Mr Shepherd complained. At other times they would turn a blind eye to the relationship. This plan fell apart because a few of the staff, not agreeing with the deception, handled events as they emerged and according to their own dictates. It then became no longer possible to 'hide' the relationship when Mr Shepherd began to visit unannounced. The result was a state of confusion for everybody and by the time an outside professional was consulted the situation had become very complicated.

Mr Shepherd became increasingly confused by the different explanations he received, once being told that he had no right to interfere. He became obsessional about visiting his wife, often leaving home before breakfast to make the hour-long journey by public transport to the nursing home. His health suffered, he lost weight, his blood pressure became alarmingly elevated and he was put into hospital.

Family members became involved. Concerned for their father, the two sons and two daughters began to visit more frequently. They had also been given various explanations about their mother's relationship with Mr X and each one interpreted the situation according to his or her own observations as well as their understanding of the nature of their parents' marriage. They felt helpless and angrily demanded that the matter be sorted out. Eventually they all agreed that action should be taken against the nursing home on the grounds of a failure in duty of care.

The situation with the staff became more complicated. When Mr Shepherd began to visit the unit at odd times, it was no longer possible to cover up his wife's relationship with Mr X. Some staff escaped when he appeared while others directed him not to visit so often.

Although management was lax in not taking action to prevent the incident from deteriorating to this extent, it was junior staff who were reprimanded and two were dismissed.

So what did the consultant do? A family conference was held, with two follow-up meetings. The true circumstances were discussed and several solutions were canvassed. Bowing to their father's wishes, the family agreed that Mrs Shepherd would be transferred to a dementia unit closer to Mr Shepherd's home. The community team arranged this without delay.

Duty of care

The concept of duty of care and its application in practice is highlighted here. Was duty of care being breached in allowing Mrs Shepherd to continue in the relationship with Mr X even though it seemed to be satisfying for both of them? Did staff have a duty of care towards Mr Shepherd or his children? Did administration have a responsibility to intervene before the situation became so entangled? Duty of care is examined in detail in chapter 9.

Similar cases, different outcomes

The following two cases illustrate different ways of handling similar situations and the impact of satisfactory and unsatisfactory outcomes. These incidents took place in separate nursing homes.

Both of the situations involved men who were married and women who were widowed. All four were in various stages of dementia. Both relationships had developed to the stage of fondling and kissing and cuddling on the bed, and they all seemed to get a good deal of satisfaction from each other's company. In both cases the moral values of staff were sorely tested; many of them had strong views that sex outside marriage was wrong and others believed that it was unnatural for old people to have a sex life. They did say that none of the four had any memory of their marriages.

Choice was another issue that bothered staff. They were concerned that the women involved had not had a chance to say 'no'. Both couples were kept apart as much as possible and when staff referred to them they frequently used terms such as 'dirty old man', 'poor little thing', 'sexual harassment', 'forcing himself on her', 'cheating on his wife' and other equally judgemental phrases.

Situation 1

The registered nurse in charge of the unit where the first couple lived was refused permission by the administration to discuss the matter with the families. The male resident was moved into another section and sedated to stop him from going back to the woman. He was so spaced out that he virtually became chairbound. The woman remained in the hostel, became melancholy and withdrawn and was prescribed anti-depressants.

This nurse said that for a long time afterwards, she was in deep conflict about the outcome of this situation. On the one hand, she had very strong beliefs about the sanctity of marriage, but on the other hand she felt unhappy about the way this old couple had been deprived of what she believed was a warm, loving relationship.

Situation 2

In the second facility a consultant was called in and she did three things. She:
• assessed the situation and satisfied herself that the relationship between the couple was not harmful to either of them
• arranged an interview — the man's wife was not in touch with him any longer, but she was able to contact the woman's daughter
• acted as a mediator between the staff, the daughter and the couple.
Staff had previously agreed that the daughter, as the mother's advocate, should have the final say about her mother. The daughter, for much the same reasons as the staff, was not altogether happy but did agree that the relationship could continue, on condition that if she or the staff were concerned at any time, they would review the situation.

The results of this second approach were seen as beneficial by everybody concerned. Staff gained a greater understanding of the couple's behaviour and by open discussion were able to change their attitudes a little towards them. The daughter for the very first time was able to perceive her mother as a sexual being. And what happened to the couple? The relationship continued quite happily for some time then, as their dementia worsened, it gently wore out.

Consent, choice and decisions

In these two cases, the issues of choice and responsibility for making a decision for a person with dementia are major issues. With whom does this responsibility rest? It also brings up questions about the rights of residents with dementia and the conflict that may exist between their rights and the rights of the institution. In this instance the pursuit of what appeared to be a satisfying contact between residents was against the policy or the ideology of the first nursing home. Institutional rights took precedence over the perceived needs of the two parties who were physically and chemically restrained to conform with the requirements of the facility. Is the insistence on residents complying with the moral ideology of the organisation sufficient justification for the use of physical and chemical restraint to force that compliance?

In the second facility there was less chance of a negative outcome because of the planned approach to the search for a solution and the involvement of all of the interested parties. However, where inflexible and conflicting attitudes and wishes pose significant obstacles to open discussion, consensus or a satisfactory result will always be difficult to achieve.

Labelling

One of the undesirable factors in both of these cases was the use of derogatory labelling ('dirty old man' and so on). Labelling pigeonholes a resident as someone to be at best tolerated and will often lead to the social isolation of that person. It is also worth noting that the labelling in these cases was only applied to the men, possibly another indication that there are often different and at times opposite attitudes towards the sexual actions of men and women despite the fact that the behaviour being assessed or judged is similar.

Unwanted attentions

Not all relationships between residents sit comfortably with both parties, nor in fact with other residents in a facility. It is not an uncommon occurrence for residents who are aware of affectionate behaviour between two of their number to react with scorn, disapproval or complaint to staff. They may reject one of the couple, or both, with other residents at times following this example even though they may be relatively unaware of their reasons for doing so. When this happens, there is a compounding of negative attitudes and 'unhappy' interactions that becomes a major and often disruptive issue for the whole facility and needs to be confronted without delay.

As far as couples themselves are concerned, it is not hard to discern whether each of them is 'happy' in the relationship or whether there is a disaffection for the other's attentions. Such was the case in a situation concerning an eighty-seven-year-old widow of three husbands, who seemed determined to acquire a fourth.

This lady was thought by staff to have a nurturing relationship with a resident in his sixties who, as well as being affected by dementia of the Alzheimer's type, had had an intellectual handicap since birth. She fed him at mealtimes, put a jumper on him when it was cold and took it off when he was too hot; at night-time she would help him undress and tuck him up in bed and generally mother him. Staff became suspicious that her attentions were not all maternal when one afternoon he ran out of his room naked, with the woman in the same state of undress pursuing him along the corridor. They found that she had undressed him and herself and made explicit sexual advances to him. He, not fully understanding, had panicked and tried to escape. Because there continued to be so many positive factors in this relationship, the only action staff took after fully assessing the situation was to supervise them more carefully in an attempt to prevent a similar occurrence.

In this incident neither one of the couple had living nor involved family. Both had legal guardians who were quite agreeable for the facility to take whatever action they thought fit, placing the responsibility firmly with the nursing home. In this particular nursing home, part of that responsibility in such circumstances is to routinely advise relatives or guardians of a problem or the steps that have been taken to deal with it.

Sexual abuse

It would probably be going too far to interpret this woman's behaviour as sexual abuse, considering the severity of her dementia, the fact that she seemed driven by impulse, and that there was an habitual element in most of her behaviour. Sexual abuse is probably one of the most emotive issues in dementia care, and can be particularly problematic for professionals and family alike. Such was the dilemma of a counsellor called into a dementia unit to sort out a three-way relationship, where a woman resident was said to be asking for intercourse with two male residents. The counsellor judged the woman to be an abuser because of her assertiveness in seeking out the men. This professional's ability to assess the situation objectively was complicated by her strong identification of the men with her own dead father and her feelings about how she would have reacted had this been him. She assumed that they were as horrified as he would have been at being 'chased' by a woman for sex.

Situations where the person is being abused by someone who is still mentally alert are usually much easier to assess and deal with, such as in the case of Mr Baxter (see page 105). Not only was Mr Baxter fully aware of his actions but there were also several signs that Mrs Baxter was distressed by his attentions. Anxiety and distress are very often the reaction of women or men who are being abused sexually or otherwise, but the situation is somewhat clouded with the passive person who is unable to communicate that sexual attentions are undesirable and unwanted. Sexual abuse is discussed more fully in chapter 10.

All of the issues canvassed in this chapter have to be taken into account when planning to intervene in situations that involve liaisons between residents and all of the circumstances handled in a way that is sensitive to everybody involved. When sorting out situations involving sexual or relationship problems where several people are concerned or potentially involved, the outcomes are more likely to be successful if the real-life partner or family, whichever is appropriate, is included. Do not overlook the wishes and desires of the partners but remember that the over-riding concern should always be for the well-being of the resident.

Ethical

and

legal issues

Ethics, law and aged care

This discussion* is from a practice viewpoint rather than a theoretical one and focuses on the ethical and legal issues involved in
the duty of care of service providers in the aged care field. Aspects
of aged care and health care are usually interwoven but when
ethics and legality are discussed in these fields, particularly in the
area of health, the discourse is usually directed towards medical
procedures and treatment. Here I have attempted to broaden this
base by applying ethical principles and legal sanctions to the general care and life quality of aged people in residential care as well
as those receiving community support.

The conduct of the professional aged careworker providing services to clients and their families involves a dynamic network of
social, psychological, medical and legal issues. Moral or ethical
considerations are also intricately interwoven with every aspect of
service provision and care. However, in determining the quality of
care for patients, clients and residents it is more likely that ethical
considerations will guide the day-to-day actions of professional
careworkers, rather than legal sanctions. In the following chapter,

* For theoretical background to this discussion the author has accepted the texts of
Mitchell et al. (1996) and MacFarlane (1995) and recommends these texts for further reading.

implications of ethical conduct and legal issues associated with
sexual activity and behaviour are discussed.

The law
Generally speaking, law consists of rules to regu-
late society made by parliament, and the rules that
have grown up through customary use (common law), all of which
are enforceable by courts of law.

There is sometimes confusion among careworkers between the
function of the law and the nature of ethics, but there are distinc-
tions. Fundamentally ethical conduct is a matter of decision for the
individual professional or organisation, whereas the legality of
actions to do with treatment and care of service recipients is determined by the law with liability (whether civil, criminal or both) for
wrongdoing. Another significant difference is that while ethical
considerations underpin the rules and regulations of many laws,
law has little to do with determining what is or is not ethical. In this
regard there are some current laws that would be considered by
many people to be unethical.

Ethics
Various schools of ethical thought pose different
theories and assumptions and the debate on ethics
is ongoing. What follows is one approach to what constitutes
ethical conduct.

Ethics deals with the nature and function of morality and is
associated with a set of beliefs, values and principles. Ethical conduct is directed towards the well-being of people and in every day
practice ethical considerations determine how the 'good' and 'bad'
or the 'right' and 'wrong' of our actions are evaluated. Our ethical
or moral beliefs also influence the way we judge the actions of
others and provide a guide for the way in which we conduct our
own relationships with other people, including our working relationships. Ethics is the basis for the standards of practice of most
professional disciplines. For example, social workers, psychologists,
medical practitioners, nurses and other professionals have individual codes of ethics which provide moral guidelines for the way

members should carry on their practice (see Appendix 3). Professional codes of ethics invariably address such issues as confidentiality and truth, the autonomy, dignity and integrity of the individual and culture-specific issues, and provide a framework by which the making of decisions about professional service can be justified. While it is self-evident that many cultures have different beliefs, values and customs which will influence the concept of ethical conduct, it is suggested that the following principles regarding the ethics of health and aged care are universal and can be shared by everyone regardless of their background.

Autonomy

The ethical principle of autonomy specifies the right of the person to make his or her own decisions about health care, voluntarily and without coercion, including the right of refusal after being acquainted with reasonable information about the treatment, procedure or prescription intended. In the present climate where litigation is becoming more common, court decisions have upheld the right of a person to refuse treatment and damages have been awarded to plaintiffs where the court has decided that insufficient information has been given about the proposed treatment. The principle of autonomy embraces the concepts of shared decision making and self-determination and in aged care service provision this principle should be expanded to mean self-regulating decisions about various aspects of the person's own lifestyle.

Informed consent

The law recognises a person's right to conduct his or her own affairs, providing they are considered competent to do so. Where medical treatment is concerned the health professional has a duty of care to give patients reasonable information about a medical diagnosis, medications to be prescribed, suggested treatment and alternatives to that treatment. The associated risks of that medication and treatment must also be clearly explained. If an allied professional believes that this information has not been adequately explained to a person in a manner they can understand by the attending physician or other person responsible, then that professional has an obligation to see that this is done. It must be emphasised that informed consent is more than a signature on a form and in order to reach the point of consent more than a few minutes explanation is often required. Informed consent should be viewed as a process of shared information, with client autonomy interacting with the skill and knowledge of the service provider. In many situations the process of shared decision making can be lengthy, particularly where there is a range of alternatives with competing options of a serious nature, and where the outcome of the treatment is uncertain. In some cases before consent can be said to be 'informed' ongoing discussion and at times counselling may be necessary.

Veracity

Truthfulness and honesty are essential elements in the process of informed consent and are indeed the basis of the trust that is necessary for the development of an effective working relationship between the professional worker and the client or resident. Professional workers have a responsibility to make sure that the information or advice given to a person is accurate and truthful about all matters relating to proposed actions and other associated matters. In the case where a person is deemed to be incompetent, such as in dementia, the same rule applies to the person's representative or advocate. Being truthful does not mean brutal frankness in the giving of information, but rather implies a sensitivity in the telling and a consideration of any seriously adverse consequences that the information may have for the recipient.

There should be little difficulty in adhering to the principle of autonomy when the competent aged person requires medical treatment or care while living in the community, or is resident in a nursing home or hostel. Unfortunately this is not always so. There is sometimes a tendency to assume that people are incapable of making calculated choices simply because they are old and frail. In such circumstances, decisions may be made for them by a worker or a family member with little or no consultation. It is also commonplace in some facilities to carry out 'minor' treatments, or psychological type 'therapy', without adequate or even any explanation to the resident. Such was the case with a ninety-year-old resident who was subjected to an enema despite her quite vigorous protestations, only to find that the wrong person had been 'treated'. There are several exceptions to the necessity of obtaining the informed consent of the resident or patient, for example when there is a life-threatening emergency or when the person is unconscious or otherwise unable to give consent. In these situations the permission of a relative should be sought or, depending on circumstances, notified as soon as possible.

Decisions affecting a person's lifestyle can have as much impact on one's well-being as those which are associated with physical health. The pressure for bed space has led to hospitals making major lifestyle decisions such as transferring competent aged persons to nursing homes, with subsequent distress for the patient who is only advised after all arrangements have been made. Alternatively if the arrangement is made only in conjunction with the family, when the patient is sufficiently competent to weigh up the issues of ongoing care, that patient can hardly be said to have been given the opportunity to consider alternatives or otherwise to have contributed to the decision. With the introduction of higher fees for entry into the nursing home system, more consultation will be necessary, at the very least regarding financial matters, and the practice of not ascertaining or ignoring the competent patient's wishes about continuing care will be more difficult, if not impossible.

Autonomy in residential care
The principle of autonomy becomes somewhat blurred when we apply the concept of choice and right of refusal to lifestyle areas of the competent resident's life. At what level does the person have the right to self-regulation? In a residential facility does someone not wanting to join a certain activity or sit near another resident whose eating habits are messy, or eat a disliked food, be firmly

'persuaded' to comply to fit in with the routine or requirements of the facility? Or be wheeled reluctantly to a place or an activity that is chosen by care staff on the grounds that it is 'good' for the resident, when he or she has expressed a wish to rest on the bed or listen to music? Should someone be heavily sedated to the point of deprivation of reasonable life quality in order to prevent wandering into another's room? Restricted in the making of certain friendships because staff or family do not approve? Deprived of the opportunity to share a bed with a resident spouse? Denied occasions for intimate moments with a visiting life partner? While these issues may seem unimportant when compared to some of the more serious matters of medical care, they often have a more marked effect on the quality of life and well-being of the person who is in a residential facility.

Autonomy and the person with dementia

Where someone is considered to be incompetent, such as in the case of a person with dementia, informed consent and self-determination are major issues. Is the person able to understand the implications and consequences of an action and able to make a decision on a considered basis? When the need for a decision of some complexity or when legal factors are involved, it is essential to ascertain that the person is in fact incompetent, and that the comparative levels of incompetence and competence are assessed. It has been known that when a long-term resident of a nursing home is observed to deteriorate mentally or emotionally over time, a superficial diagnosis of dementia may be made, when in reality the appearance of dementia may be due to other causes, often reversible.

The distinction between what constitutes an irrational choice and what constitutes an incompetent decision must also be critically evaluated. A choice which may appear somewhat bizarre or does not make sense to the careworker or with which the worker strongly disagrees is often taken as a sign of incompetency, whereas in fact, however irrational it may seem, it may well be a choice made according to the person's beliefs and wishes. The measure of incompetency has to do with cognitive defect or intellectual incapacity rather than rational or emotional reactions.

A diagnosis of dementia is very often equated with a global inability to make choices or reasonable decisions, whereas incompetence in dementia can range over a continuum from partial incompetence to total incompetence. Someone in an early or mild stage of dementia, for example, may still be able to make a relatively complicated judgement, such as that associated with the negotiation of an enduring power of attorney, or the expression of detailed directions and wishes about his or her care when and if home care is no longer an option. A person who is in a severe stage of dementia, for example, Alzheimer's disease, may not be able to indicate even the simplest wish. The capacity for reasonable decision making will to some extent depend on the type of brain involvement, the degree that the disease process has advanced, and the type of choice being considered. A person affected by dementia may be able to make a decision which fits in with the definition of legal competency, such as fully understanding the process and implications of making a will or she or he may be able to make certain lifestyle choices. But another person may not have sufficient judgemental capacity to weigh up the complicated issues and consequences of say, the removal of a brain tumour or the social and financial implications of a transfer to another facility. Someone affected by dementia who is unable to fully appreciate the pros and cons of the need for surgery or the consequences of treatment, might well be able to consent to say, dental treatment for a raging toothache.

Note: Assessments of a person's competency must always be carried out by a trained and experienced professional.

Empowerment

There is now an emphasis on people maximising the control they have over their lives. The concept of empowerment is just as valid for the person with dementia as for others and that empowerment should be to the extent that the person can reasonably use. No matter how right or beneficial for the recipient the careworker believes a proposed action is, the principle of autonomy, however limited in the case of dementia, must not be overlooked.

The person with dementia should always be given the opportunity to express agreement or disagreement to any proposed action from playing bingo to forming an intimate relationship. If that person is unable to reasonably contribute to a decision that will have significant consequences for her or his lifestyle then that person's advocate, usually a family member or friend, should be consulted. Regardless of the degree of comprehension, talking about the proposed action or procedure with the person with dementia is desirable. The capacity to understand may be better than it superficially appears and the person may have the ability to indicate approval or disapproval or agreement or disagreement. And while it may not make an appreciable difference to a serious decision or to the assessment of legal competency, this practice is not only desirable in recognising the integrity of the person, but is one that also fits marginally with the ethical principle of autonomy.

There is a conviction in some organisations that the responsibility for making most, if not all decisions about the care, treatment and direction of dementia residents, other than those who are under the guardianship of the Public Guardian, rests solely with the organisation. This can mean that a number of different people with a wide range of training and experience are in the position of making choices for residents, or different choices for one resident, particularly the type of decisions that impact on the resident's lifestyle. This practice also applies in some circumstances when a dementing person lives alone in his or her own home. In New South Wales, the *Guardianship Act 1987* (and similarly in other states) includes a section specifying authority for consent to medical and dental treatment. This section covers all persons over the age of sixteen years who are unable by reason of injury, mental illness or intellectual disability to give consent to treatment and sets out the authority for consent:

a) the guardian, where there is a guardianship order with respect to the incompetent person

b) the spouse (including de facto spouses) where there is no guardianship order

c) the person who has care of the incompetent person where neither of the above applies.

Many aged care organisations and professionals use this section as a guideline in circumstances where a decision is necessary, particularly with regard to those matters that are, or might be, contentious in nature. While outside of medical and dental treatment they are not required by law to do so, they consider it ethically desirable to involve partners or other family members where appropriate, and where possible the person with dementia.

Lifestyle choices

A person with dementia who is not able to make complicated or valid judgements about major aspects of his or her life may well be able to express a choice about day-to-day activities and relationships. Even where there is little or no verbal skill, wishes, likes and dislikes can be graphically expressed and can often be understood by a family member or a careworker who is familiar with a resident and the person's particular pattern of communicating.

In New South Wales the Office of the Public Guardian sets out the following vision statement, which can be seen to be based on the ethical principle of respect for the person to make self-regulating decisions:

> The Public Guardian believes that people with impaired decision-making ability have the right to the widest range of choices possible concerning how they meet their lifestyle needs and manage their affairs. The Office of the Guardian is committed to maximising those choices.

Do good and do no harm

These two ethical principles are also called beneficence (do good) and non-maleficence (do no harm).

Health and aged care professionals have a moral obligation both to the service recipient and to society to do the best they can in their caring roles. Depending on their level of knowledge and expertise, they have a duty of care to ensure that their interventions will result in a benefit to the person being cared for and by extension they must not engage in any action that will pose a risk of harm, or damage to any person in their care. Even though a harmful action may not be intentional, if that action causes damage or injury to the person, then in some circumstances the worker can be held responsible. Duty of care regarding doing good and doing no harm also extends to failure to provide a reasonable standard of care or to an omission to carry out an appropriate procedure. For example, the worker who fails to carry out any task or action that is necessary for a person's well-being and that which complies with an expected standard of care to a patient, client or resident could be considered by law to be negligent and so to have done harm.

The person with dementia

The principle of doing good and not doing harm takes on a special significance when associated with the day-to-day care of people who are affected by dementia. Because of perceived impairment in the capacity to make choices and in expressing wishes, careworkers feel obligated to decide what is 'good' or 'not good' for people with dementia. Most professional workers strive to fulfil their duty of care by acting in what they consider to be the best interests of patients, clients and residents, and do not intend that their interventions will harm them. However, as pointed out earlier, the careworker is not always the best person to decide what is or is not a 'good' intervention for clients or residents. This is largely because of differences in beliefs and experience, not understanding the nature of old age, the ignoring of the person's wishes and the influence of the worker's position of power.

Short-term 'good', long-term ...?

The implementation of the ethic of 'doing good' can sometimes be a complex process involving not only attention to the good or harm that is involved in taking certain actions and but also balancing the relative good and harm of such actions. This is outlined in the following situation.

> A dementia careworker supported the doctor's advice to the family not to tell a relative of a diagnosis of Alzheimer's disease, made on the grounds that it would cause extreme anguish (harm) to the patient and that it would be more humane to conceal the nature of the illness (good). This action might meet the requirement to do good in the short term (say prevent the risk of depression), but in the long term may have negative effects and so do harm. In not advising the person of his condition he is screened from perhaps the urgency of making a current will, contributing to decisions about his future care, making arrangements about finances and business matters or assigning an enduring power of attorney. The long-term consequence may be that his spouse or next of kin is eventually left with a messy social and legal situation that in itself will cause considerable strain and stress and may result in a serious decline in the quality of life of the couple. With the loss of control of cognitive abilities and not having negotiated an enduring power of attorney, the dementing person may squander the family finances either through gambling or generously bestowing gifts, lose the ownership of his property or make unreasoned business decisions that can lead to litigation. All of which have been experienced by families.

Whether or not to give a person with dementia information that may have a significant effect on his or her life is a dilemma that continually confronts professional carers. Does the person have a right to know? In situations such as these the duty of care associated with the giving of information to the patient or resident and how much should reasonably be given needs serious consideration, taking into account evaluation of all the circumstances.

Telling about the death of a partner

Another issue with which the dementia careworker is often faced is informing a resident about a death. A decision is often made not to tell the dementing resident of the death of a spouse or other 'close' visitor because the careworker finds it too difficult to discuss death or is apprehensive about his or her ability to deal with the person's pain. Sometimes a family member will decide that the person not be told. This decision is mostly made on the consideration that it is kinder not to tell: 'He'll soon forget ...', 'Anyway she doesn't know who ... is now'.

It may well be futile to advise someone of a death when the dementia has progressed to a stage where people have little or no awareness of what goes on around them and there is little response to other people. However, there are those who, while confused about the identity of a partner and no longer remembering the nature of the relationship, will nevertheless have had a strong emotional tie with the person who has died. Even though there might be no reaction immediately after this tie is broken, after some time the bereaved person may react to the absence in a variety of ways.

While in the short term the decision not to tell may be in the best interests of a resident, in the long term it may have the opposite effect. The dementing person may begin to have catastrophic reactions, pacing and wandering sometimes to the front door of the unit, or other familiar places shared with the now dead person. Anger, whimpering, crying and deep depression (or other signs of a catastrophic reaction) can also follow the continued absence of the familiar person as can other uncharacteristic behaviour. For example, some weeks after the death of her husband a woman who had not been heard to use words for a long time, began pacing around the unit day and night, crying out his name. Because of the time lapse between the time of death and the behaviour, grief is often overlooked as the contributing factor to these reactions. It has been observed that even though the person with dementia is grossly confused, the 'normal' feelings of grief can be experienced, although they may not be able to be verbalised. The person with dementia has as much need as others to experience these feelings and to be supported to the greatest possible extent through the time of crisis.

When it is better not to tell

However, not everyone has the same reaction to the news of death. There are times when not emphasising the death of a loved one is the most desirable path to follow. This is particularly so when the dementing person is unable to accept the fact of the death, often reacting violently to the news, and sometimes mentally replacing the dead person with another relative, friend or member of staff.

Take the case of an eighty-eight-year-old woman who in quick succession lost her only brother, husband and home and was moved to an aged care hostel.

> She was unable to accept the reality of the death of her husband, despite staff repeatedly telling her. A normally gentle person she became aggressive and at times violent, and was severely restrained, both physically and chemically. The main exception to her disturbed behaviour occurred during the visits of her son-in-law, who she happily recognised as her dead husband. Staff strongly advised the family not to go along with her 'delusion', directing them to reinforce the staff action of emphasising the husband's death — 'She has to come to terms with reality'. It would have to be considered that this woman was reacting to compounded grief which she was unable to understand or articulate. Her confusion was being further exacerbated by the conflict between what her dementing brain was telling her and what professional carers were insisting she believe. As is the case with many people with dementia she was communicating her feelings in the only way she knew how.

In situations such as this and for the well-being of a dementing person, it is essential that careworkers learn to accept the 'reality' of the disturbed mind and try to step into and understand the confused world of dementia.

Justice   The principle of justice or fairness is fundamental to
the conduct of most professionals and of aged care
organisations where there is commitment and adherence to ethical
principles. Ideally the principle of justice is enshrined in the
pol-icy of the organisation in terms of equity of service and non-
discrimination on the grounds of race, gender, social class, financial status or religion. The outcome standard for planning and
leadership as set out in the principles of the *Aged Care Act 1997*,
states, 'The organisation has documented the residential care
service's vision, values, philosophy, objectives and commitment to
quality throughout the service' and this should help service
provider organisations to focus on the ethical basis of their service
(if they have not already done so) including that of fairness in
service provision.

Confidentiality

While confidentiality is not an ethical principle it is a rule, usually explicit, associated with all dealings between a professional careworker and the receiver of the service and interacts with all other
ethical principles, and with the concepts of honesty, trust and the
right to privacy. When someone is assured that personal information will not be revealed to others, they feel safe in confiding that
which would otherwise remain private. In some organisations,
however, confidentiality is held to be between the client or resident and the organisation, not the individual worker, and where
this policy exists it should be made known to the person being
interviewed. In the provision of care, sharing of information is
more often than not desirable, even necessary, for the benefit and
well-being of the person. If information is withheld because of fear
of the consequences of it being shared, it may be to the detriment
of the person being cared for.

Implicit in the necessity to share certain information with other
service providers is the responsibility of the careworker to advise
the client or the client's representative when this is the situation.

The advice should be given before a confidence is revealed, together with an explanation of the benefits.

Confidentiality also applies to records. No information that will lead to 'grapevine gossip' or which is not necessary for the care or treatment of the resident or client or which will 'harm' the person in any way should be recorded. However, there are provisions that legally override the confidentiality of information in certain circumstances. For example, it is a legal offence to conceal a crime. Confidentiality does not apply:

- when there is knowledge that a serious crime has been committed (S.316, New South Wales *Crimes Act*)
- in some situations associated with a person's well-being (to prevent harm or injury to that person or another).

Ethics embodied in law

An example of law which is based on ethical principles, rules and concepts are the standards as set in Schedules 2–4 in the Principles associated with the Commonwealth *Aged Care Act 1997*, from which the following extracts are taken:

(Residential Care Principles)

- Residents' physical and mental health will be promoted and achieved at the optimum level in partnership between each resident (or his or her representative) and the health care team.
- Residents retain their personal, civic, legal and consumer rights, and are assisted to achieve active control of their own lives within the residential care service and in the community. Outcome standards included in this principle:
  - Each resident receives support in adjusting to life in the new environment and on an ongoing basis.
  - Residents are assisted to achieve maximum independence, maintain friendships; and participate in the life of the community within and outside the residential care service.
  - Each resident's right to privacy, dignity and confidentiality is recognised and respected.

- Each resident (or his representative) participates in decisions about the services the resident receives, and is enabled to exercise choice and control over his or her lifestyle while not infringing on the rights of other people.
- Residents live in a safe and comfortable environment that ensures the quality of life and welfare of residents, staff and visitors.

(Community Care Principles)

- Each care recipient and prospective care recipient (or his or her representative) is to have access to information to assist in making an informed choice about available community care services.
- Each care recipient is to receive quality services that meet his or her assessed needs.
- Each care recipient (or his or her representative) is enabled to take part in the development of a package of services that meets the care recipient's needs.
- Each care recipient should be enabled where possible, and encouraged, to exercise his or her preferred level of social independence.
- The dignity and privacy of each care recipient are to be respected, and each care recipient (or his or her representative) will have access to his or her personal information held by the provider.
- Each care recipient (or his or her representative) has access to fair and effective procedures for dealing with complaints and disputes.
- Each care recipient will have access to an advocate of his or her choice.

An example of questionable ethics

Look again at the situation that involved Mr and Mrs Shepherd discussed in chapter 8. It is worth examining the conduct of the staff and management of the nursing home in the light of ethical principles and concepts.

The significant feature of this situation was the breach of ethical conduct through the deception of the staff of the nursing home regarding the relationship between Mrs Shepherd and Mr X. A group of staff deliberately conspired to take action that was intended to mislead and deceive Mr Shepherd and subsequently his adult children. Staff most probably justified this action on the grounds that their responsibility was to the well-being of the residents and that it was the couple's right to form their own friendships (doing good). But repeatedly separating the couple when the family visited in an attempt to 'cover up' resulted in the two residents acting out their distress in a way that risked their physical and mental well-being (doing harm). It seems that the reason for the initial deceitful action was because of the difficulty in initiating a discussion with Mr Shepherd, his wife's representative, before the situation got out of hand. When it did, a senior staff member attempted an explanation, but by that time Mr Shepherd was too anxious or depressed to take in what she was telling him (information was not given so that he could understand). As time went on layer upon layer of deceit contributed to an undesirable and complex situation with unpleasant consequences for, and harm done to, everybody involved. The couple was permanently parted and so deprived of a friendship, Mr Shepherd's health was seriously affected, the family was upset, staff were dismissed and the nursing home was confronted with a threat of legal action.

While the Shepherd case is extreme, similar situations are experienced in a number of residential facilities and, possibly with the duty of care towards residents in mind, are handled with too little thought for the consequences. Liability for conduct that is misleading or deceptive is now enshrined in Australian law and theoretically Mr Shepherd would have had a legal case. However, it is still unclear how this law relates to persons who are the receivers of health, welfare and care services through community agencies and residential facilities.

CHAPTER
10

Knotty issues

Anybody who shares the care or fully cares for a person with dementia will appreciate the complexity of sorting out the mix of emotions and opinions, expectations and wishes that surface in almost every aspect of the life of the affected person. Even where the desire of everyone is to enhance the dignity and lifestyle of the person with dementia, there can be a variety of expectations and ideas even within the family as to what is best for the affected person. When a service provider is involved, the ideas of the family carer may differ from those of a professional careworker, or be contrary to the practice of the organisation providing the service. When it comes to matters of sex and intimacy, untangling the threads can become an even more complicated exercise involving conflicts of perceptions, attitudes and wishes already discussed at length.

Four knotty issues are explored in this chapter: the gathering of sexual information, rights, the use of restraint and sexual abuse. In studying these issues, I have listened to the opinions and feelings of partners, families and careworkers and canvassed the practices of service providers.

Gathering information Currently there is a groundswell of opinion among careworkers that it would enhance the well-being of everyone involved if attitudes about sexuality of old people, including those who are affected by dementia, were more enlightened. Some service providers have suggested that in order to better understand the intimate needs and sexuality of old people, a question about sexuality should be included in the assessment procedure. This could be at the time of contact with the Aged Care Assessment Team, residential care facility or community service agency. While this seems to be a good idea, it does bring up a number of issues. What sort of information is being sought? Does the worker have the right to ask for information about a person's sex life? Does the person with dementia or his or her representative have a responsibility to disclose information about sexuality or behaviour that might adversely affect the lives of residents of care facilities and staff? How does a person's right to privacy fit with a request for disclosure of sensitive information? How does the service provider approach the matter?

Entitlement to information

The only information that the care organisation or the professional careworker is morally entitled to is that which will impact on the care and well-being of the prospective client or resident or of other residents, and that which is relevant to the service being offered. For example, information that is necessary for the well-being of a person in residential care may be entirely different from that required by an in-home respite worker.

Another factor to be considered is the case where information is voluntarily offered, but which has no bearing on the care of the client or resident. In such instances the worker has some responsibility to protect the teller from a disclosure that he or she might later regret. Contact with a care agency is usually at a point of crisis for the family caregiver and no less for many prospective residents. For most caregivers it is a time of great vulnerability and in situations where the interviewer is empathetic and the interviewee is distressed, she or he may blurt out all sorts of private thoughts or relate experiences of an intimate sexual nature. At a later time the recollection of an uninhibited confidence may generate considerable guilt and there is always a risk that it will constrain the relationship with the careworker, even to a point where the client is too embarrassed to consult that person again – 'Whatever will she think of me?'.

When there are indications of the premature telling of a confidence, the professional carer has an obligation to interrupt, 'Excuse me, but I wonder if you really want to tell me this just now. I'm quite happy for you to go on, but maybe you'd like to think about it for a day or two'. The person who is being interviewed now has a choice. On the one hand, he or she might decide that the relief from sharing innermost thoughts far outweighs any other consideration. On the other hand, a moment to pause and reflect may lead to a decision to abort or delay the confidence. If that information becomes significant at a later date, the careworker can always reintroduce the subject. 'A little while ago you started to tell me ... I think the time has come when we need to know this. Do you feel as though you can talk about it now?' A comment like this can be followed or preceded by an explanation as to why the information is now of interest.

Responsibility to disclose information

Family carers or service recipients (where possible) have a moral responsibility to divulge whatever information is considered necessary to enhance the ability of careworkers to act for the wellbeing of the client or prospective resident. I have found that when approached with a professional and sympathetic manner, people are usually generous in supplying information even though they might sometimes appear to be reluctant to do so. Apart from the embarrassment of talking about sex, the apparent reluctance can be a response to the stress of the occasion. For instance, on the day of admission to a residential facility, the home caregiver's or prospective resident's attention is often concentrated on the intense emotional impact of the reality of nursing home care. Sometimes, too, nursing home admission can bring with it extreme distress as a result of the realisation of the finality of the person's condition.

Another factor that has to be taken into account is the personality of the client or carer. A socially reclusive or unconfident person or one who is suspicious of authority can be overwhelmed by having to disclose such personal information to a stranger. If the interviewer is able to demonstrate concern and compassion, over time people will usually feel sufficiently secure to freely disclose all necessary information.

The benefits of information

Where it is the policy of an organisation to meet the needs for affection and sexual gratification of couples, it is desirable that the subject of intimate needs is raised at the first comfortable moment. The facility then has the opportunity to establish whether it is the couple's wish to continue their intimate life and advise them of organisational arrangements for the provision of space and privacy. Information of this type also indicates how the facility will meet the resident's needs for warmth and affection and is of particular importance when the resident does not have a partner, or is no longer part of a close relationship.

In the case of prospective residents (either permanent or respite), a day club participant, or where a home respite worker will be spending time alone with a service recipient, it is essential to know about any behaviour that is of a deviant or sexually harassing nature. This sort of information forewarns the professional carer or the facility and gives them an opportunity of responding to the behaviour in the most appropriate way, if and when it occurs.

Initiating discussion on sexual matters

Many careworkers find it difficult to initiate a discussion with people much older than themselves on matters of sexuality either because of the right of the person to privacy or embarrassment on the careworker's part. Some old people, too, can feel uncomfortable when asked to discuss sexual matters. The following vignettes are typical of responses to two questions randomly raised with thirty-one carers of people with dementia. These responses illustrate the attitudes of both home caregivers and residential careworkers in talking about sex and intimacy.*

Question 1: How would you feel if [nursing home staff] asked questions about your wife's/husband's/partner's sexual behaviour?

> **Wife aged sixty-six:** I wouldn't want to talk about it. When we got married we made a promise to each other that we'd never talk about what went on between us, not in bed, not to anyone. Even though he wouldn't know about it, I'd feel like I'd broken my promise to him — almost like being unfaithful.

> **Husband in seventies:** Well, I understand that they might want to know all about her, but why sex? I don't understand that. I don't think I'd feel too comfortable talking about it with someone I'd just met even though they're a professional. Probably go to Dr X, he's known us for a long time, and get him to give them the stuff they want. Although it might be different if I'd known them [nursing home staff] for a while and knew if I could trust them or not.

> **Woman aged fifty-five:** No I wouldn't talk about it. I'm gay and I know how some of them [staff] treat gays in nursing homes. Where I work they talk about them behind their backs; it's even worse when someone is out of their mind because they can't stick up for themselves and they often get insulted to their faces. This freaks them out; I've seen them get violent because of the way some staff throw off at them and then they get tied up [physically restrained] or put on pills [tranquillisers] until they are bombed out of their minds. I'll look after her at home, I won't put her in a nursing home, so I don't have to think about answering any of their questions.

* From professional contacts with the author.

For different reasons all of these carers show a determined reluctance to discuss sexual behaviour in all of the above situations. None understood the type of information that would be sought nor the use to which it would be put, nor did they enquire. Even though the partners in the first two examples gave different reasons for their reluctance to talk about sexual matters, there is a strong feeling from both that they put a very high value on their privacy.

The wife indicates that she feels strongly that any disclosure about the couple's sexual life would amount to a betrayal of the trust she and her husband had enjoyed in their relationship. She would undoubtedly have some feelings of guilt if she spoke about their intimate life. If the necessity arises for the husband's sexual behaviour to be assessed, the offer of counselling to the wife prior to such a step being taken would need to be considered.

There is a chink in the expression of reluctance from the husband in the second example. He qualifies his discomfort by saying he would go to his doctor if such information was requested. Then again he thinks that disclosing the information might be acceptable if he could trust the person seeking it. Obtaining the information through a third party with the permission of the partner, or the prospective resident, does however offer an alternative to direct interview where embarrassment or other reasons for strong reluctance are factors. What actually did happen when this husband was asked to give information of a sexual nature is related on page 148.

The third partner illustrates an entirely different set of circumstances. Although this woman was not sure why details about intimacy would be required, her own life experience and the attitudes of staff in the particular nursing home where she worked as a chef made her strongly opposed to divulging any information of an intimate nature.

While a person should not be pressured in any way to confide personal information, if this information is considered essential at the time of interview, it could be helpful to enquire about the reason for the reluctance. 'I know it's never easy to talk about these very private things, but do you have a special reason for not wanting me to know? Can you talk to me about it?' An enquiry such as this can often be sufficiently reassuring for the interviewee to feel more comfortable. At the very least it allows the careworker to explore the circumstances of the unwillingness.

Following is an imaginary scenario of the way a careworker might conduct this part of an interview at the point of admission to a nursing home. We assume that before this part of the interview, the careworker had already introduced the idea of sexuality and explained why the information was requested.

Worker: I get the feeling that you're holding something back.

Spouse: Why do you say that?

Worker: Well because when I asked you if there was anything particular you would like to tell us about her sexual behaviour, you said 'Not really'. I know this is something that can be very hard to talk about to someone else, but I just wondered what 'not really' meant.

Spouse: My wife is a very private person and we never talked about this sort of thing, even to each other and I know she'd be horrified if she thought I was talking like this to you. And I think I have a right to protect our privacy, don't you? There are privacy laws aren't there?

Worker: Yes there are, and I think that it is very hard for someone like you who has always protected their privacy to be asked to break the habit — especially with a stranger — and I guess my age doesn't help either. But anyway, if there is anything else that might help us with caring for you wife I would really appreciate it if you would let us know.

Notice that when the spouse resists her enquiry, she does not press him for the information, rather she respects his feelings about his right to privacy and recognises that it is difficult for him to talk about sex. When he communicates his discomfort with this discussion, she picks up on his embarrassment with words that imply sexuality and avoids using such terms. She also recognises that his reluctance might be partly due to her youth. Undoubtedly having reflected on this interview, this man might feel more comfortable in providing at least some information or to return, either to talk about his wife's sexual behaviour, or affirm that there is nothing to tell, whichever is appropriate.

Question 2: How did you feel when they talked to you about your sexual life?

> **Husband:** Well, as you know I'm a pretty shy sort of person and I didn't see what that had to do with looking after my wife in a nursing home. But the little nurse who was asking me the questions, she was a real doll and really understood how I felt ... I didn't feel at all embarrassed. She explained that sometimes when people with dementia like my wife go into a nursing home their sexual urges can get out of hand, just like the other ways they change. She said it would be better if they knew if there had been any changes in her — well — you know — sex, so that they'd understand her better. So I told her that [wife] had been really leaning on me lately for sex — more than she used to before she got sick. Well she said she could give us some privacy if I wanted. I was glad about that. She told me too ... sometimes two patients [residents] would get to be close friends — I think she meant more than friends — because they might mistake another man for their husband. I don't know how I'd feel about that, but I'll cross that bridge when I come to it. But at least I'm prepared for the worst. Anyway, she [wife] has a private room and we can do what we like when the door's closed.

The nurse gave this carer a satisfactory explanation for her enquiries saying that it would help staff to understand his wife. The carer responded so positively that he appeared to have no difficulty in offering information about his wife's changed sexual impulse and seemed quite comfortable in accepting the news from the nurse that he would have an opportunity to have sex with his wife in a private room. The nurse alerting him to the possibility of his wife bonding with another resident, at least prepares him if and when such an occasion arises. With somebody else, this latter information might have been better left to a later interview but in this case the atmosphere of the interview obviously indicated to the nurse that it was 'safe' to discuss this with the spouse.

So how did this twenty-four-year-old nurse introduce the subject of sex? She reported that the latter part of the interview went something like this:

> **Nurse:** Thanks very much for being so patient, I know it's not easy to remember all these details. If you think of anything else we should know to make your wife comfortable here, please come and tell me about it. There's just something else before you go. You know sometimes when somebody comes into a nursing home, everything is so different and you remember how I said that they can often change in the way they act — well sometimes this applies to some sorts of behaviour that we'd probably call sexual. Sometimes their sexual urges get out of control. It only happens with a few people and probably won't happen with your wife, but if you can think of anything that she might do that we should know about, we'd like to know about it.
>
> **Husband:** I don't think there's anything ... only ... it's a bit hard to talk about this, it's a bit private.
>
> **Nurse:** Take your time, I know it's not easy to talk about your private life.
>
> **Husband:** Well ... she's changed a bit the last six months ... in bed, if you know what I mean ... Wanting me to go to bed with her more than she used to ... all times of the day and night ... even followed me into the garage the other day asking me to do it ... [laugh] ... I'm a bit past all this, getting on a bit.
>
> **Nurse:** It sounds as though it's getting a bit much for you.
>
> **Husband:** Well ... no, not really, we still enjoy it.

Nurse: How would you feel if I could give your wife a private room as soon as one is available. We try here to give husbands and wives some privacy so that they can have time together without other people around. How would you feel about that?

Husband: Yeah, it's a relief. I was really upset when I couldn't look after her any more. I thought that's the end of our marriage, and I wondered how she would get on without me. Yes that makes me feel better. Thank you, thank you.

Nurse: Well thanks very much for being so cooperative. Is there anything else you would like to ask me?

Husband: No, nothing I can think of now.

The following situation was not handled as well.

Wife: I was angry — it came like a bolt out of the blue — fancy talking about sex at my age! She was asking me all sorts of questions. Well I know that was to help them to understand him — you know sickness and drugs and things and what he liked to do with his time and all. Suddenly she just said, 'How's your sex life?'. Well I told her that that was my business. I was so embarrassed and she just kept saying that they had to know. Well I was frightened that if I didn't tell them, they wouldn't take him, and I couldn't think of anything. So I told her about the trouble we used to have when we first married and how we couldn't have children for ten years and I told her what I used to do to get him going and she had a bit of a giggle and wrote it all down. I feel so ashamed. I was embarrassed having to tell this to someone who is not much older than my grand-daughter. I hate going back there and I'm trying to have him moved to somewhere where they aren't so nosey.

Some people react positively to a direct question, while for others confrontation with an issue that is embarrassing for them or which is opposed to their morality can be offensive. It is fairly obvious, that the question about sexuality was embarrassing this woman, although it might not have if the subject had been introduced more gently. Under the circumstances it would have been better if the worker had not pursued it at that time. Not fully understanding what was required and under pressure, the wife poured out information about her early married life which had nothing whatever to do with the care or well-being of her husband or any other resident. Even so, had the careworker interrupted her and empathised with what was a very painful period in this woman's life, her embarrassment may have dissipated and an angry reaction might have been averted. Rather the wife gained the impression that the interviewer was amused (it may have been embarrassment) and she became concerned that what she was saying was being written down.

This woman's experience also brings up the issue of the fear that many carers experience – that the service of the facility will be withdrawn if they do not comply with an organisational request. Many a carer remarks, 'I don't like to complain in case they take it out on him (or her)'. Any such impression implied by a facility is not to be tolerated.

> **Daughter aged forty-five:** It was absolutely necessary to tell them. Mother and father are a real Darby and Joan; she loves him dearly and can hardly bear to be parted from him. Even though she knows it is going on, she pretends it's not happening. So when he went to the day club, I felt that it was up to me to tell them. It all started about a year ago when I went into his room one day, and he pressed up against me. Then it got to a stage when he'd try to put his hand down my front or under my skirt. But, you know, he knew enough not to try it when mother was in the room. I knew that he'd been 'losing it' for some time, and I just accepted that this was part of the deterioration, that he couldn't control himself any more — he'd always been a sexy guy — and that I would just have to handle it the best I could. I thought that he would only do this with me, but I brought a colleague home one day, someone he'd never

seen before, and he just walked up to her and cupped her face with his hands and said, 'You know you have the most kissable mouth'. And for the rest of the time she was there, he never took his eyes off her. The old scallywag was trying to seduce her right there in front of us, and he wasn't being too subtle about it either. After that it happened with some of my other friends too, so you see why I didn't have any hesitation in letting them [the day club] know. Anyway they were very pleased I told them and they handle him very well. What do they do? Well he's okay when he's playing active games like quoits or going for a walk or something like that, but when they do things where they sit down, or at lunch, they always sit him between two men. The lady who supervises them is pretty good at controlling him; she's very firm with him when he tries anything on.

Woman aged sixty-five: I have this understanding social worker in the community team and she knew that I was having a bit of trouble with [partner] and she's been helping me to manage it. He'd been making some rude suggestions to our young grandchildren that worried me a bit. It wasn't too bad while he was at home, I could manage it, I just didn't leave him alone with the kids. But now he's going into the dementia hostel, I didn't quite know what to do about it. You know I didn't want them to think that he was really like this, it's only happened this year. Well, she's going to let them know, she'll be able to explain it better than me and she can tell them that we aren't really married and that'll be a load off my mind too.

Social worker: I've known her since her husband was first diagnosed with dementia — that's about three years ago. They've been together now for about thirty years, never married because his first wife won't divorce him — divorce is against her religion. It's been a happy arrangement; they have two daughters and a son and five grandchildren. I don't think they ever consider they're not married except in cases like this, when they have to front up to strangers. Then it's pretty hard for her.

So it'll make it easier for her because she's already out of her mind with anxiety about the way he's going on with the children. It'll make it easier if I can give a report to the dementia unit and then she can take her time in talking about it to them. About the way he's been acting towards the children? Well she first noticed it about six months ago, and for a long while she wouldn't talk about it, she felt so ashamed to think he would do this — talk about sex to them. It was only when she found him fondling one of the little ones that she panicked and agreed that everyone would be better off if he went into residential care. I know this place and they will handle his behaviour very sensitively. Of course it mightn't happen with adults.

When a sexual problem is suspected

Sometimes there is a suspicion that a domestic problem is being caused or exacerbated by sexual behaviour and there are indications that the client is unsure about raising the matter. In circumstances like these, she or he can be greatly relieved if the worker introduces it. A psychologist approached such an issue in this manner with a client.

The couple had been referred to him by the community team about a year before because of some disagreement in the family about the father's dementia. He saw the wife fortnightly to help her cope with a very difficult situation. She then started popping in every couple of days on one pretext or another and he suspected that something else was causing her anxiety, although she vehemently denied it. 'No', she said, 'everything's fine'. After about three weeks, on one of the unscheduled visits when the opportunity arose, he said, 'Well, I've got a hunch that you might be having a spot of bother with the way [husband] is acting sexually. And I think you're finding it hard to talk to me about it'. Her denial was a little less forceful and the following day she telephoned and tearfully made an appointment to discuss 'a matter'. She confided that her husband's sexual impulses had become uncontrolled and several times during the past weeks he had raped her after physically overpowering her.

In this example, the psychologist had some previous knowledge of the husband's heightened sexual impulse and he was alerted to the wife's anxiety by her unscheduled visits without apparent reason. His 'hunch' or educated guess was enhanced by the assessment he had made after dismissing other possible concerns which he had explored with the wife on her unscheduled visits. The benefit of this gentle and sensitive approach is that the client does not feel pressured to divulge information that she was not ready to confide. The client is reassured that the therapist respects her right to privacy and understands her unreadiness to talk about an embarrassing matter.

Whose rights?

Probably the most contentious issue in dementia care, particularly in nursing homes and dementia-specific hostels is the question of rights (see Appendix 1) and no more so than in matters of sexuality. While valuable guidelines are provided in statements which set out the rights and responsibilities of residents, organisations and workers, the practicalities of balancing the rights of the resident, family, staff and organisation is a delicate operation that can be fraught with difficulty. Even informal discussions on how rights should be determined constantly raises more questions than there are answers. For example, the generalisation that each case should be judged on its merits invariably raises the question, 'Whose merits?'. In the process of determining what and whose rights should take precedence, particularly where there is a difference of opinion, a number of competing priorities have to be weighed. With no ethical or practice guidelines about sexuality and relationships to depend on, the decision as to whose rights will prevail is often made by snap moral judgement.

Priorities for the handling of 'sexual' relationships in residential care are often established for reasons of 'sound management' alone and while this may be organisationally satisfactory, it may not be so for the resident or the resident's family. In some facilities, decisions about sexual issues are left to careworkers and are often driven by the attitudes of the person who is seen to hold a position of power, regardless of whether that power is formal or informal.

Although there is now a trend to empower service recipients to make their own informed choices, the person with dementia is relatively powerless. Arbitrary decisions to deny needs for sexual fulfilment and intimate companionship are inevitably made without reference to the person with dementia, even though the person may obtain and express pleasure as a consequence of a close relationship or gratification of sexual desires. Every effort should be made to determine the resident's needs and wishes.

Rights in residential care

Organisations are of course entitled to establish rules which are based on their particular doctrine and moral values. When residents and families have the same moral attitudes as those of the facility, matters of sexuality are usually fairly uncomplicated. But what of situations where institutional rights clash with those of a resident and the family or representative? When there is a conflict of morality, sometimes the right of a 'well' spouse to make decisions for the affected partner will create difficulties for the facility, as this Director of Nursing of a dementia-specific unit relates:

> We have a policy here to recognise that some of our residents have sexual needs and to try to meet those needs if we can. We had an awful problem with this man [Mr B]. He was pretty obviously frustrated — chased anyone and everyone for sex. So open about it too, just put the hard word on any female at all — staff, residents and even visitors. I tried to talk to his wife about it, because I thought if I gave them some privacy that they'd have some time to be affectionate, even to make love if they wanted to. I thought this might be the answer. Well she absolutely refused to believe that he would want sex, kept telling me,

'Fornication is evil when it's used purely for pleasure' and
repeated over and over, 'We've kept strictly to our beliefs all of
our married life, we've abstained since I went through the
change of life', and she said that there is no way that she was
about to change. Actually on a couple of occasions she blamed
us for his behaviour and once said that staff must be encouraging
him! Anyway, she wouldn't give us permission to get the doctor
to medicate (testosterone-inhibiting medication) to dampen
down his ardour. When he went on one of his 'raids', the whole
unit was in a turmoil — some of the old ladies were just terrified
of him. It got so bad that I had the option of taking it up with
the Guardianship Board or asking him to leave. Well, she chose a
transfer and he went to ... where they've got him on Serenace
[tranquilliser]. He's not interested in anything much any more.

In this situation the insistence of the spouse on exercising her right
to refuse medication to control his sexual behaviour conflicted with
the facility's right to provide a safe environment for all residents,
staff and visitors. Being unable to satisfy his sexual needs (her
right) because of her beliefs interfered with the right of her husband
to have his sexual needs met. In the second facility, the management insisted on their right to have him sedated, which having no
sexual connotation, satisfied the wife's moral values. The consequence for the resident was a denial of his rights so that the rights
of others could be protected.

When organisations have strict moral rules about sexuality and
intimacy these should be, but are not very often, disclosed to
prospective residents or the dementia resident's representative.
Organisations have a responsibility to discuss at an appropriate
time, with prospective residents or their representatives, issues of
morality particularly with regard to sexual behaviour. If it appears
inevitable that a contrast in attitudes is likely to significantly
impact on the lifestyle and well-being of the resident, alternative
accommodation arrangements can then be considered. By informing a couple of such a policy, it gives them the opportunity to seek

accommodation where they can continue what is for them an important part of their partnership. If they are not aware of the policy of non-cohabitation and these rules are unwittingly 'broken', or a resident and partner do not comply with what is considered by the facility to be morally defensible, the consequence may be that the resident is 'punished' for what, by the facility's standards, is unacceptable behaviour.

When organisational policy denies couples the opportunity for intimate sexual activity on moral or other grounds the organisation's rights prevail over those of the couple. In such cases, not only is the resident with dementia deprived of the warmth and affection of the partner, but will most probably be further distressed by the inability to comprehend the reason for a careworker's disapproval.

With so-called indecent sexual actions, a restrictive approach is often employed. For instance, when self-fondling in public is considered to be 'morally wrong', rather than because of loss of control due to the dementia, the 'offender' may be scolded, shamed, subjected to strong personal disapproval, physically restrained or finally transferred to another facility. Any one of these methods of control has the possibility of severe emotional and psychological cost to the resident and to the partner. With regard to the rights of the 'offender' whose behaviour is controlled by such restrictive means, we would have to query not only the denial of his right to sexual satisfaction so that the rights of the organisation can be accommodated but also his right to be treated with dignity. Alternative ways of handling these sorts of situations (see chapter 5) should always be considered as long as they do not deny the rights of the person or other residents. Note, however, that the moral rights of the organisation, and some staff, might still be infringed.

The chef (see page 145), who had a gay companion, worked in an institution where homosexual relationships were considered to be sinful, and although this was not explicitly stated, the administration made no attempt to control the undesirable reactions of staff towards a homosexual resident. While the administration of this particular facility (and others) would never deny or qualify the principle that everyone in their care had a right to dignity, there was a thinly veiled attitude in this case that, as sinners, homosexual people did not have rights.

Regardless of sexual preference or whatever the nature of the sexual partnership, a person has an entitlement to residential care if and when the need arises. While some organisations are opposed to unmarried sexual relationships or homosexuality, there are other facilities where it is not an issue. When seeking residential accommodation, sexual preference or other matters that might impinge on a prospective resident's lifestyle can be discussed with the Aged Care Assessment Team where an appropriate facility can be recommended.

Who decides?

When dementia is a factor and in the absence of guidelines to handle situations with a sexual component, management and staff response protocol varies from place to place. In practice it is often the case that the one who lays claim to 'ownership' (staff, facility, representative, guardian) of the resident considers that they are entitled to make the decision on how a situation should be handled. Where there is no organisational policy to handle sexuality, often individual staff are left with the difficult task of deciding whose rights are to be protected and how this should be done. The Public Guardian, while accepting responsibility for consenting to medical and dental treatment and decisions about appropriate care, does not intervene in 'relationship' matters of those under their guardianship and some residents' representatives are agreeable to leave most, if not all, decisions to the facility. Other family members or residents' representatives believe that decisions as to what is best for the person on whose behalf they are acting is their sole responsibility, as in the case of Mr B above. When there is a conflict of attitudes and opinions, then firm priorities of competing rights may have to be established.

In previous chapters we have discussed several situations where conflict of rights is a major issue. In this situation, the administration of the facility enforced its right to intervene in the relationship between the two residents, ignoring the right of the family to be informed or to contribute to a plan of action. There was also a conflict between the administrative decision and what the registered nurse saw as her professional responsibility to provide quality care to the two residents. The rights of the two residents were completely overlooked, particularly 'to select and maintain social and personal relationships with anyone else without fear, criticism or restriction' (Charter of Residents' Rights and Responsibilities, Schedule 1, Sections 23.14 and 23.16, *Aged Care Act 1997*, Commonwealth of Australia).

Use of restraint

Another issue is the common practice in some residential facilities of using physical restraint and psychotropic drugs to 'manage' behaviour (see Appendix 4).

Physical restraint

The practice of physically restraining old people for whatever reason has been described at one end of the scale as a protective technique and on the other end as a barbaric practice. The results of the latest Australian research (Retsas, 1997) indicate that in South Australia approximately one third of nursing home residents are physically restrained, while overseas figures cited by Retsas suggest that between 4 per cent in the United Kingdom and 43 per cent in the United States are subject to this form of control. There is mounting opinion worldwide against the use of physical restraint. Results of international research suggest that it does not achieve the outcomes intended, for example, preventing falls, but rather that a number of undesirable health problems can be the consequence of this practice. At the extreme end of risk is the statistical evidence that restraint was the cause of one in every thousand nursing home deaths in the United States due to strangulation from restraining straps.

Restraint

Physical restraint is the restriction of a person's free body movement or normal access to the body by the use of such devices as straps, lap trays, vests, bed rails and bean bags or gerichairs that are difficult to get out of, and restraint by the use of physical force.

Chemical restraint is when drugs are used to control behaviour and is defined in the discussion paper, 'Report of the NSW Ministerial Taskforce on Psychotropic Medication Use in Nursing Homes, May 1997 as:

> Chemical restraint is the use of medication to control a person's behaviour when no medically identified condition is being treated, where the treatment is not necessary for the condition or amounts to over-treatment for the condition. Chemical restraint includes the use of medication when the behaviour to be affected by the medication does not appear to have a medical cause and part of the intended pharmacologic effect of the drug is to sedate the person for convenience sake or disciplinary purposes.

Consent: All medication requires consent in New South Wales. If a person is unable to give consent then the 'person responsible', usually the spouse, must do so. Psychotropic drugs are classed as major medical treatments and if to be used regularly, must be prescribed by a doctor with written consent of the 'person responsible'. Occasional use by staff when considered necessary can be initiated by a doctor.

Chemical restraint

When behaviour is seen to be a problem, drugging residents is often the chosen method of control and in some places sedation is the automatic choice for dealing with many behavioural situations. Prescription of psychotropic drugs is sometimes at the insistence of the facility and from considerable anecdotal evidence and observation, appear to be used on many occasions for the convenience of staff rather than for the well-being of the resident or the protection of other residents, although it might be justified as such. Occasionally a spouse distressed by the partner's attraction to another resident will request that he or she or the other resident be 'given something' to interrupt the relationship. However, staff of facilities where there is a 'no restraint' policy report that while at times there is difficulty in negotiating other means of resolving problem situations, an agreeable solution is invariably reached.

While physical restraint is often used with the person who engages in what is considered to be self-expressed sexual behaviour, such as self-fondling or masturbation, chemical restraint is the chosen method in some places to control 'sexual' harassment and to intervene in 'illicit' relationships. The use of drugs or physical restraint to intervene in a relationship between two residents with dementia, merely on the grounds that it is not morally acceptable, in itself must be considered as unethical and immoral especially given that many of these relationships never proceed past the hand-holding stage. The following are responses from senior staff from different residential facilities during discussion on the effectiveness of the use of restraint to control close relationships.

Staff 1

We don't seem to have too many problems and we have quite a few who have what you'd call a relationship. They sit together and look after each other. Most of it's pretty innocent.

Sometimes you get the pair who want to jump into bed together every time they get the chance. If they seem happy together and there aren't any family involved, we look the other way. But you've got to be very aware of how the husbands and wives feel, it's an awful shock to some of them. They're just devastated to think that someone they have been with for sometimes fifty years, can just forget them and go off with somebody else.

Staff 2

> We found that a lot of our staff — they're all fairly young — were pretty critical of residents who got together like this, especially when they're married [to someone else]. Mind you it doesn't happen very often in our nursing home because we don't have many residents who are mobile. Because I'm pretty short-staffed, I don't have the time to supervise staff continually, and I started to get complaints about the way that some of them were treating the dementia residents who were getting over friendly. So it seemed like the lesser of two evils to dampen down their ardour early in the piece [relationship]. I get the local doctor to prescribe a sedative prn [as required] any time that we see something like this starting up — although I don't always tell him exactly what it's for in case he refuses.

This last situation emphasises several dilemmas: shortage of staff; difficulty in obtaining trained staff, particularly in rural communities; the lack of on-the-spot staff training to deal with these sorts of issues; the pressure on medical practitioners to prescribe sedatives and tranquillisers at the request of a facility. Although not specific to this situation, some medical practitioners report that if they refuse to prescribe medication prn at the request of a facility, they know there will be another doctor who will. The possibility then exists of losing patients who may have been treated by that practitioner for many years.

Staff 3

> Well I have very strong views about this! Marriage is marriage and just because a [dementia] resident doesn't remember he's married, doesn't alter the fact that he is married. I take very strong action if any of my patients [residents] start any of that hanky panky. If I can't keep them away from each other, they go straight on to a sedative. Our doctor understands the problems we have with sexual harassment. I don't have to do this very often because I can usually separate them. We have two units

and I just move one into the other part of the hostel. There's no excuse because I let all of my patients have as much privacy as they like with their wives.

When dementia residents are mobile, which is the case in most dementia-specific units and some nursing homes, wandering into rooms of residents of the opposite gender and lying on beds is often considered to be sexually motivated. Except in rare circumstances, the male wanderer is not reacting to sexual impulse or even acting purposefully, but nevertheless women residents can be terrified by such an intruder. To use drugs to restrain the wanderer who has no idea that he is in forbidden territory and who poses no risk of harm to anyone, in order to prevent another resident from becoming frightened, seems quite illogical as well as unethical. Yet this is not an uncommon reaction of management to this sort of situation. (See chapter 8 for other ways of handling this sort of behaviour.)

Of course there are circumstances where the administering of sedatives and tranquillising drugs is the only effective and justifiable way to control behaviour, such as in the rare instance of extreme and continuous aggression, violence or agitation when other techniques have failed, and when safety of the person or others is at risk. However, most problems, including determined sexual harassment, can be handled more effectively and humanely.

Abuse The abuse of older people is attracting increasing concern among aged careworkers. Australian researchers in the forefront of addressing elder abuse, Kurrle et al. (1991), define elder abuse as, 'the wilful or intentional harm caused to a person by another person with whom they have a relationship implying trust', and this definition has been widely accepted.

Abuse includes the infliction of physical pain or injury; psychological abuse through intimidation or purposeful indignities; financial abuse by improper control of the person's money and property; and sexual abuse. Results of studies (Kurrle et al., 1991) generally suggest that people with dementia are more likely to suffer from physical and psychological abuse than other old people and that women are more likely than men to be abused.

One of the main obstacles in obtaining a true picture of the extent of abuse of older people is the lack of a precise definition of what constitutes abuse. Whether the behaviour is judged to be abusive is often dependent on the beliefs and values of the person making the assessment and on the different social, cultural and family framework within which the behaviour occurs. This uncertainty is reflected in the various institutionalised protocols for handling situations where abuse is a factor. The section on human rights in the discussion paper on Elder Abuse and Dementia prepared by Elizabeth Weeks and Paul Sadler for the New South Wales Advisory Committee on Abuse of Older People, 1997, indicates a range of different opinions as to whose rights should be paramount in cases of abuse. For example, the Guardianship Board operates under the principles of the Guardianship Act which states that the interests of a person with dementia must come first while the NSW Police Service indicates that the rights of the victim must take precedence. This poses an immediate conflict in such cases, for example, where children were being abused by a dementing grandfather and a woman had been brutally raped by a husband with dementia.

Other agencies such as the Alzheimer's Association and Aged Care Assessment Teams emphasise the rights of the carer to be protected from abuse by the dementing family member and the need for all the circumstances to be taken into account, not only the abuse. These factors alone illustrate how complex is the matter of handling abuse of older people. It is recommended that legal processes should be engaged only as a last resort, after all other avenues to resolve a problem situation have been exhausted.

Sexual abuse

The definition of sexual assault and abuse of older people widely accepted in Australia also comes from Kurrle et al. (1991), 'Sexually abusive or exploitative behaviours ranging from violent rape to indecent assault and sexual harassment'. If the problems in dealing with abuse of a physical, psychological and financial nature of people with dementia are complicated, those of sexual abuse are even more so, imbued as they are with conflicts of morality, values, attitudes, wishes, choice and ageism. Evidence of sexual abuse associated with dementia is hard to come by; there are no serious bruises, black eyes or money missing from bank accounts and disturbed behaviour is overlooked as a consequence of sexual abuse. The paucity of information creates difficulties in establishing the true extent of the problem. Most statistics indicate that sexual abuse of people living in the community is rare: as little as 2 per cent of all cases of identified abuse.

Because anecdotal evidence suggests that sexual abuse is more frequent than this, it is possible that the true extent of this type of abuse remains hidden in the community for a number of reasons. There may be a reluctance or inability of the person with dementia to expose the abuser or, where there is a history of abuse in the relationship, she or he may have become accustomed to this sort of behaviour. Another factor is the difficulty in establishing who it is that is being abused, the person with dementia or the carer, or whether the assessment of what constitutes abuse is in terms of the intent of the suspected perpetrator or in the perception of the person being abused.

While in the home, the sexual abuser is invariably a partner or a close acquaintance, in care facilities, particularly where all or many of the dementia residents are mobile, the 'abuser' is likely to be another resident. However, it is not uncommon for staff to identify certain visitors, usually male, whose purpose they suspect is solely to obtain sexual gratification from a woman resident with whom they are acquainted. Of course the question arises as to whether a woman is being abused if she accepts the sexual overtures of either the visitor or another resident and is obviously obtaining pleasure from the experience. The person with dementia will usually react quite strongly when rejecting unwanted advances from others. More difficult to assess is someone, either man or woman, who is passively and habitually accepting of all contact with other people. Any sign of distress or change in the usual way that a person acts probably indicates discomfort, such as in the situation with Mrs Baxter (see page 105).

Sexual abuse of carers

From stories told by carers of people with dementia, the indications are that sexual abuse is not an uncommon experience and that it is sometimes accompanied by other forms of violence from the person being cared for. Some carers talk of continual and determined insistence on sex by the affected partner while others, more rarely, tell of experiences of physical overpowering and rape. In some of these relationships there is a long history of abuse involving extreme sexual submission of the carer. Advancing age and frailty makes this situation all the more intolerable. In other partnerships the sexually harassing actions appeared only with the advance of the dementia.

Sexual abuse of staff

It must often seem to residential staff that they are one of the few groups of employees, or the only group, where part of the job is to be subjected to both verbal and physical abuse. The prime example of staff abuser is the dementia resident, usually but not exclusively male, who sounds off with a string of lewd language and disgusting suggestions and makes indecent advances to staff of the opposite sex. A typical ploy of this type of male abuser is to manoeuvre a female worker into an inescapable corner of the shower recess and make determined sexual advances.

Administrative opinion as to how these situations should be handled ranges from excluding junior staff from this task to training them how to handle this type of behaviour. Sometimes, though, the solution is not so straightforward. On a recent consultancy in a dementia unit, an anxious seventeen-year-old personal care assistant asked for an interview and related with graphic detail how a male resident tried to rape her every morning when she was showering him. So why didn't she tell her supervisor? She understood that it was part of her job to handle such situations and, what was more, in the country town where she lived jobs were hard to come by and she could not risk losing her job by appearing to be incompetent. Encouraged to discuss this with her supervisor, the task of showering this man was transferred to a more senior nurse.

Note   The above section on sexual assault should be read in conjunction with other sections of the book dealing with matters associated with abuse and harassment. In addressing the topic of sexual abuse, rather than suggesting answers and solutions, the purpose is to stimulate discussion about sexual harassment and assault in both residential facilities and in the home.

An essential document for aged care workers is *Abuse of Older People* which was produced by the New South Wales Advisory Committee on Abuse of Older People – Inter-Agency Protocol, October 1995.

SECTION

4

Exercises

These exercises are designed to be used in small or large group discussion, for the setting of assignments at various levels of training, or for self-learners to test their knowledge. Some lend themselves to role-play in small groups.

Section 1: Sexuality and old age

1   What is meant by sexuality and sensuality?

2   Myths stereotype people. What are some of the myths that have developed about sexuality and old people?

3   Take the myth, 'Old people are not sexually attractive'. Why do you think this might be wrong? Include in your discussion the part the media plays in reinforcing this myth.

4   List some of the emotions that careworkers experience when dealing with old people. Can you add to this list from your personal experience?

5   Read the list of behaviours on page 17. What attitudes could make these behaviours difficult to cope with?

6   Are there any 'sexual' behaviours that you might have difficulty with? Why?

7   What are some of the reasons why old people could feel embarrassed to talk about sex?

8   Why do you think that some old people are reluctant to be showered or toiletted by careworkers?

9   In what ways do you think your experience of growing up differed from that of people who are now in their seventies?

Section 2: Sexuality and dementia

1 How might sexual behaviour change when someone is affected by dementia?

2 Some people with dementia have an increased demand for sexual gratification. What are some of the factors that could contribute to this behaviour?

3 Sexual values and attitudes are often retained regardless of the effects of dementia. How could this affect behaviour?

4 What is a catastrophic reaction?

5 How could you help to prevent a catastrophic reaction?

6 What is disinhibited behaviour?

7 In what way/s could you meet the needs of love and affection for a person in your care?

8 What are some of the reasons that the 'sexual' behaviour of a person with dementia might be different in residential care compared to home?

9 Behaviour that is often considered to be sexually motivated is not always so. What other reasons could there be for 'self-expressed intimacy' such as masturbation, self-fondling, and 'exposure' in public?

10 List some actions of careworkers that could inadvertently trigger sexual behaviour?

11 Name the three steps of the problem solving approach.

12 What are the advantages of the problem solving approach?

13 Read some of the stories in chapter 7. Explain how dementia can alter the balance of a partnership and how family and friends can support the caregiving partner.

14 Adult children can be affected by a change in the relationship of parents. How might they react to these changes?

15 Some of the staff in your workplace are mocking a couple who are openly affectionate. What would you do?

- join them
- keep quiet
- object to the way they are behaving
- ask your supervisor to bring the matter up for discussion.

16 Many new residents have difficulty in settling in to an unfamiliar environment. What could some of the reasons be?

17 It is not unusual for two people with dementia in residential care to form affectionate relationships. Why do you think this is so?

18 Explain how a life partner might feel and react when a spouse is accepted into residential care.

19 Read situations 1 and 2 on pages 108–109. What are some of the effective ways in which staff responded in those situations?

20 What are the consequences of labelling people?

Section 3: Ethical and legal issues

1   What are ethics? In what ways do ethical principles influence the way we should act?

2   The three ethical principles are:

   • autonomy or respect for the person to make decisions

   • do good and above all do no harm

   • justice.

   Name at least one way in which one of these principles might influence your work with someone with dementia?

3   A relative confides something to you in confidence and you think this information might be important for the general well-being of the dementia client or resident. What do you do?

   • Tell the relative you will keep the confidence?

   • Explain that you will share the information with other staff?

   • Try to explain that you will share the information with other staff before the relative confides the information?

   • Say nothing?

4   Discuss the Shepherd case on pages 112–114 in relation to:

   • ethical principles

   • support for staff by management

   • intervention by a social worker consulted by the family

   • the careworkers.

5   When might you want information of a sexual nature about a client or resident?

6   You work in a dementia-specific hostel. A married resident has formed a close relationship with another resident. How would you tell the spouse about this relationship? What words would you use to initiate the discussion?

7   Most of us believe that everybody has rights. Whose rights do you think should take priority in residential care? Describe a

situation you have experienced where there has been a conflict of rights or use a situation in this book to illustrate your point.

8 Why do you think that drugs and physical restraint are not desirable methods to control behaviour?

9 In your residential facility there is a male resident who wanders aimlessly. Sometimes he wanders into the rooms of female residents and lies down on their beds. They are frightened. What are you going to do about it?

10 You suspect that a woman you have been visiting in her home is being sexually abused. What steps will you take:

• to find out if your suspicions are correct?

• to handle the situation if they are?

11 It is not uncommon for dementia careworkers to be subjected to sexual abuse. What would you do if this situation occurred where you work:

• as a careworker?

• in a supervisory position?

APPENDIX 1:
Residents' rights and responsibilities

User rights and responsibilities for community care

23.25 Rights of care recipients

(1) A care recipient has the following rights:

   (a) to be involved in deciding the community care most appropriate for the care recipient's needs;

   (b) to be given enough information to help the care recipient make an informed choice;

   (c) to choose, from the community care available, the community care that best meets the care recipient's needs;

   (d) to be given a written community care plan of the community care that the care recipient will receive;

   (e) to receive community care that takes account of the care recipient's lifestyle and cultural, linguistic and religious preferences;

   (f) to be able to take part in social activities and community life as the care recipient wishes;

   (g) to be treated with dignity, with the care recipient's privacy respected;

   (h) to complain about the community care being received, without fear of losing the care or being disadvantaged in any other way;

   (i) to choose a person to speak on the care recipient's behalf for any purpose.

(2) The approved provider must not act in a way inconsistent with the care recipient's right to enter into a community care agreement with the provider.

23.26 Rights of prospective care recipients

(1) An approved provider must give written advice to a prospective care recipient, or the care recipient's representative, about the rights, responsibilities and entitlements of the care recipient and provider, including the care recipient's rights and responsibilities about payment of community care charges.

(2) The advice must be given before confirmation of the date for the start of the community care.

Aged Care Act 1997 – Principles – Part 3

Charter of residents' rights and responsibilities

A. Each resident of a residential care service has the <u>right</u>:

- to full and effective use of his or her personal, civil, legal and consumer rights

- to quality care appropriate to his or her needs

- to full information about his or her own state of health and about available treatments

- to be treated with dignity and respect, and to live without exploitation, abuse or neglect

- to live without discrimination or victimisation, and without being obliged to feel grateful to those providing his or her care and accommodation

- to personal privacy

- to live in a safe, secure and homelike environment, and to move freely both within and outside the residential care service without undue restriction

- to be treated and accepted as an individual, and to have his or her individual preferences taken into account and treated with respect

- to continue his or her cultural and religious practices, and to keep the language of his or her choice, without discrimination

- to select and maintain social and personal relationships with anyone else without fear, criticism or restriction
- to freedom of speech
- to maintain his or her personal independence
- to accept personal responsibility for his or her own actions and choices, even though these may involve an element of risk, because the resident has the right to accept the risk and not have the risk used as a ground for preventing or restricting his or her actions and choices
- to maintain control over, and to continue making decisions about, the personal aspects of his or her daily life, financial affairs and possessions
- to be involved in the activities, associations and friendships of his or her choice, both within and outside the residential care service
- to have access to services and activities available generally in the community
- to be consulted on, and to choose to have input into, decisions about the living arrangements of the residential care service
- to have access to information about his or her rights, care, accommodation and any other information that relates to the resident personally
- to complain and to take action to resolve disputes
- to have access to advocates and other avenues of redress
- to be free from reprisal, or a well-founded fear of reprisal, in any form for taking action to enforce his or her rights.

B. Each resident of a residential care service has the responsibility:

- to respect the rights and needs of other people within the residential care service, and to respect the needs of the residential care service community as a whole

- to respect the rights of staff and the proprietor to work in an environment free from harassment
- to care for his or her own health and well-being, as far as he or she is capable
- to inform his or her medical practitioner, as far as he or she is able, about his or her relevant medical history and current state of health.

Aged Care Act 1997 – Principles – Sections 23.14 and 23.16

APPENDIX 2:
Rights and responsibilities of workers

The following has been reproduced from the *Legal Issues Manual* prepared by the NSW Advisory Committee on Abuse of Older People, September 1995, with permission from the NSW Government, Department of Ageing and Disability.

It appears the law is often viewed by workers as something frightening. In fact the opposite is true as the law provides a framework of assistance and a measure of security for workers and clients alike. Many workers, especially those in health-related areas, are concerned about contact with the legal system, because it is an area with which they are unfamiliar. This is slowly changing and workers are beginning to see the law as another avenue by which they can assist the people they see.

Workers' rights

- Workers have the right to physical safety and a safe system of work.

- Workers have a right to support and information from their agency or department. Employers have an obligation to their workers to provide appropriate legal advice and support.

- Workers have a right to be informed by their organisation of the organisation's protocol for dealing with situations of abuse.

Workers' responsibilities

- Workers have a responsibility to their clients to provide competent professional assistance.

- Workers have a responsibility to be aware of their organisation's complaints mechanism and to assist people to lodge a complaint if they are not satisfied with the service provided.

- Workers have a responsiblitiy to follow agency and interagency protocols endorsed by their agency as a standard of best practice.

APPENDIX 3:
Social workers' code of ethics

The following extract from the Social Workers' Code of Ethics © is reproduced with the permission of the Australian Association of Social Workers Ltd.

Value statement

- Every human being has a unique dignity irrespective of nationality, ethnicity, social and economic status, gender, sexual preference, age, beliefs or contribution to society.

- Regardless of its form each society has the obligation to pursue social justice, protect its members from harm and provide maximum benefits for all.

- Each individual has the right to self-fulfilment provided that the rights of others are not violated.

- Every social worker has the responsibility to devote objective and disciplined knowledge and skill to aid individuals, groups, communities and societies in their development and in the management of conflicts and their consequences.

- Every social worker has the primary obligation to the objective of service, this taking precedence over personal interest, aims or views.

Principles of practice

3.1 Commitment to social justice
The social worker will advocate for changes in policy, service delivery and social conditions which enhance the opportunities for those most vulnerable in the community.

3.2 Development of knowledge
The social worker will take responsibility for expanding, identifying,

developing, using and disseminating knowledge for social work practice.

3.3 Relationship with employing organisation
The social worker will relate as a member of the social work profession to the employing organisation.

3.4 Confidentiality and privacy
The social worker will respect the privacy of clients and hold information obtained in the course of professional service in confidence except where the law demands otherwise or there are ethical or moral reasons not to do so.

3.5 Client self-determination
The social worker will make every effort to foster maximum self-determination and social responsibility on the part of clients.

3.6 Service
The social worker will give priority to the service obligation of the social work profession.

3.7 The integrity of the profession
The social worker will maintain and develop the purpose, principles and practice standards of the profession.

3.8 Competence and professional development
The social worker will maintain and strive to improve proficiency in professional practice.

3.9 Professional conduct
The social worker will maintain high standards of professional conduct.

Standards of practice

4.1 Commitment to social justice
The social worker will act to prevent and eliminate discrimination against any person or group on the basis of race, gender, sexual orientation, age, religion, national origin, marital status, political belief, mental or physical disability or any other preference or personal characteristic, condition or status.

The social worker will act to ensure that all persons have access to the resources, services and opportunities which contribute to their well-being.

The social worker will act to expand choice and opportunity for all persons with special regard for disadvantaged or oppressed groups and persons.

When acting for clients the social worker will consider the implications for the competing interest of others.

The social worker will promote policies, practices and procedures that encourage respect for the diversity of cultures which constitute Australian society.

The social worker will encourage informed participation by the public in shaping social policies and institutions.

4.2 Development of knowledge

The social worker will base practice upon knowledge relevant to social work.

The social worker will maintain a critical approach to new knowledge.

The social worker will participate in continuing education programs following graduation.

The social worker will contribute to the knowledge base of social workers and share research knowledge and practice wisdom with colleagues.

The social worker engaged in study and research will be guided by the conventions of scholarly inquiry.

The social worker engaged in research will consider carefully its possible consequences for human beings.

The social worker engaged in research will ascertain that the consent of participants in the research is voluntary and informed without any implied deprivation or penalty for refusal to participate and with due regard for participants' privacy and dignity.

The social worker engaged in research has responsibility to protect participants from unwarranted physical or mental discomfort, distress, harm, danger and deprivation.

The social worker who engages in the evaluation of services or cases will discuss them only for professional purposes.

The social worker will take credit only for work actually done in connection with scholarly and research endeavours and credit contributions made by others.

Identifying information obtained about participants in research will be treated as confidential.

4.3 Relationship with employing organisation

As an employee, the social worker will recognise the stated aims of the organisation, contribute to the development of its policy and work towards the best possible standards of service to the client.

Where policies or procedures of the employing organisation contravene professional standards, the social worker will endeavour to effect change through appropriate organisation channels. Subsequently the support of this Association could be sought or appeal be made to other groups or the wider community.

The social worker will use the resources of the employing organisation with scrupulous regard, and only for the purpose for which they are intended.

4.4 Confidentiality and privacy

The social worker will respect the confidentiality of information obtained in the course of professional service. The social worker will not share confidences revealed by clients without their consent except when compelling moral or ethical reasons exist.

The social worker needs to inform clients fully about the limits of confidentiality in any given situation, the purposes for which information is obtained and how it may be used.

The social worker will afford clients reasonable access to official social work records concerning them.

When providing clients with access to records, the social worker will take due care to protect the confidences of others contained in those records.

The social worker will obtain informed consent of clients before their activities are electronically recorded or observed by a third party. Such records will not be used for any purpose without informed consent.

4.5 Client self-determination

The social worker will provide clients with accurate information regarding the extent and nature of the services available to them and will not knowingly withhold such information.

The social worker will apprise clients of their rights and implications of services available to them.

In circumstances where the social worker must act on behalf of a client, the social worker will safeguard the interests and rights of the clients.

When another individual is acting on behalf of a client, whether legally authorised or not, the social worker will deal with that person always with the client's best interests in mind.

The social worker will be able to justify any action which violates or diminishes the civil or legal rights of clients.

4.6 Service

The social worker will retain responsibility for the quality of social work service performed by that worker or a student/trainee under his/her supervision.

The social worker will act to prevent practices that are inhumane or discriminatory against any person or group of persons.

The social worker will not exploit relationships with clients, students and trainee social workers for personal advantage.

The social worker will not solicit the clients of one's agency for private practice.

The social worker will not exploit professional relationships for personal gain.

When setting fees, the social worker will give consideration to the client's ability to pay.

The social worker will renegotiate or terminate services to clients and the professional relationships with them when the client's interest or needs are no longer served.

The social worker who anticipates the termination or interruption of services to clients should notify them appropriately and seek the transfer, referral or continuation of services in relation to clients' needs and preferences.

The social worker who serves the clients of colleagues during a temporary absence or emergency will serve them with the same consideration as that afforded any client.

4.7 The integrity of the profession

The social worker will uphold and advance the values, ethics, knowledge and commitment of the profession.

The social worker will protect and enhance the dignity and integrity of the profession and is encouraged to be vigorous in discussion and criticism of the profession.

The social worker will make no misrepresentation in advertising as to qualifications, competence, service or results to be achieved.

4.8 Competence and professional development

The social worker will not misrepresent professional qualifications, education, competence, experience or affiliations of self or others.

The social worker will engage in practices, including continuing education, which facilitate evaluation and the development of competence in practice.

The social worker will utilise supervision/consultation during her or his practice lifetime as a means of developing practice competence.

4.9 Professional conduct

The private conduct of the social worker is a personal matter to the same degree as is that of any other person, except when such conduct compromises the fulfilment of professional responsibilities.

The social worker will distinguish between statements made and actions made, done as a private individual, and as a representative of the social work profession, an organisation or group.

The social worker will not solicit the clients of colleagues.

The social worker will not charge a fee or accept or give anything of value for receiving or making a referral.

The social worker will not assume professional responsibility for the clients of another agency or a colleague without appropriate communication with that agency or colleague.

The social worker will maintain cooperative relationships with other members of other professions and staff engaged in providing services to the client.

APPENDIX 4:
Dementia and drugs – a layperson's guide to medical jargon

The following has been reproduced with permission from the Alzheimer's Association, New South Wales and is an extract from the 'Treatment of Behavioural Complications' HelpNote produced by the Association and prepared by Professor Henry Brodaty, a psychogeriatrician and Honorary Medical Adviser to the Association.

Drug: Medication that can be prescribed by a doctor.

Side effects: Unwanted effects. These occur in a minority of patients. Listing them in the table below does not mean they will occur, merely that they may. Some are exceedingly rare. Your doctor or pharmacist can advise.

Consent: All medication use requires consent. In New South Wales, if a person is unable to give consent, then the 'person responsible', usually the spouse, must do so. Psychotropics are classed as major medical treatments and if to be used regularly, must be prescribed by a doctor with written consent of the 'person responsible'. Occasional or prn can be initiated by a doctor but consent should be confirmed later.

Dosages: Each psychotropic drug has a set dose or range of dosage at which it is effective. General guidelines are well documented, but individual patients vary. People who are older and those who have any disease affecting the brain (e.g. dementia) may be more sensitive to the drug and require less.

Generic prescribing (chemical name/trade name): All drugs have at least two names. One is the pharmacological or chemical name, e.g. diazepam, and is always written in lower case. The other is the trade name registered by the pharmaceutical company who makes it. If more than one company makes it, there may be several trade names, e.g. Valium, Ducene.

PRN: as required (Latin: *pro re nata*).

Drugs	Examples	Uses	Side effects
Anticonvulsants/ antiepileptics	*carbamazepine (Tegretol)	to prevent epilepsy, stabilise mood and reduce behavioural disturbances such as aggression	drowsiness, unsteadiness, liver abnormalities
Antidepressants: Tricyclics	*desipramine (Pertofran) *nortriptyline (Nortab, Allegron) *amitriptyline (Tryptanol) *imipramine (Tofranil) *doxepin (Sinequan) *dothiepin (Prothiaden)	treatment of depression	constipation, dry mouth, difficulty with urination, postural hypotension, sedation
Antidepressants: Tetracyclic	*mianserin (Tolvon)	treatment of depression	as for tricyclics, especially sedation
Antidepressants: MAOIs (monamine oxidase inhibitors)	*pheneizine (Nardil) *tranylcypromine (Parnate)	treatment of depression	as for tricyclics plus low blood pressure **Danger** — interacts with certain foods and other drugs to produce high blood pressure
Antidepressants: RIMAs (reversible inhibitors of monoamine	*moclobemide (Aurorix)	treatment of depression	nausea, headache, dizziness, insomnia

Drugs	Examples	Uses	Side effects
Antidepressants: SSRIs (selective inhibitors of monoamine oxidase)	*fluoxetine (Prozac) *sertraline (Zoloft) *paroxetine (Aropax)	treatment of depression	upset stomach, diarrhoea, increase in agitation, insomnia
Minor tranquillisers (sedatives)	*diazepam (Valium, Ducene) *oxazapam (Serapax) *lorazepam (Ativan) *chlordiazepoxide (Librium)	for anxiety, agitation	drowiness, difficulty concentrating, addiction
Minor tranquillisers (antipsychotics/ neuroleptics)	*thioridazine (Melleril) *haloperidol (Serenace) *chlorpromazine (Largactil)	treating hallucinations, delusions and sometimes behavioural disturbances such as aggression	symptoms similar to Parkinson's disease (tremor, stiffness, shuffling walk) which are reversible and tardive dyskinesia– a delayed onset side-effect of abnormal movements usually affecting the mouth which may be irreversible; also constipation, dry mouth, difficulty passing urine, postural hypotension
Hypnotic (sleeping tablets)	*temazepam (Normison, Euhynos) *nitrazepam (Mogadon) *flunitrazepam (Rohypnol)	to assist with going to or maintaining sleep	as for minor tranquillisers

BIBLIOGRAPHY

Aged Care Act 1997, Principles, Commonwealth of Australia.

Alexopoulos, P. (1994). Management of sexually disinhibited behaviour by a dementia patient. *Australian Journal on Ageing*, 13 (3).

Archibald, C. Sexuality and sexual needs of the person with dementia. In T. Kitwood & S. Benson (Eds.), *The new culture of dementia care*. Loughton, Essex: Hawker Publications.

Berg, A., Welander, H. U., Hallberg Ingalill, R. (1994). Nurses' creativity, tedium and burnout during one year of clinical supervision and implementation of individually planned nursing care: Comparisons between a ward for severely demented patients and a similar control ward. *Journal of Advanced Nursing*, 20.

Bird, Michael (1998). Psycho-social rehabilitation for problems arising from cognitive defecits in dementia. In R. Hill, L. Backman, A. Stigsdotter Neely (Eds.), *Cognitive rehabilitation in old age*. London: Oxford University Press (in press).

Bird, Michael, Llewellyn-Jones, R., Smithers, H. et al. (1998). Challenging behaviours in dementia: A project at Hornsby/Ku-ring-gai Hospital, *Australian Journal on Ageing*, 17 (1).

Bird, Michael, Alexopoulos, P. & Adamowicz, J. (1995). Success and failure in five case studies: Use of cued recall to ameliorate behaviour problems in senile dementia. *International Journal of Geriatric Psychiatry*, 10.

Brasch, R. (1973). *How did sex begin?* Sydney: Angus & Robertson.

Brodaty, H. (1997). Guide to medical jargon. In *The Dementia Educator*. NSW: Alzheimer's Association.

Butler, R. N. & Lewis, M.I. (1993). *Love and sex after 60*. New York: Ballantyne Books.

Comfort, A. (1976). *A good age*. New York: Mitchell Beazley.

Derouesné, C., Guigot, J., Chermat, V., Winchester, N. & Lacomblez, L. (1996). Sexual behavioural changes in Alzheimer disease. *Alzheimer Disease and Associated Disorders*, 10 (2).

Drickamer, M. A. & Lachs, M. S. Should patients with Alzheimer's disease be told of their diagnosis? *The New England Journal of Medicine*, 326 (14).

Hallberg, I. R. & Norberg, A. (1994). Nurses' experiences of strain and their reactions in the care of severely demented patients. *International Journal of Geriatric Psychiatry*, 10.

Hellen, C. R. (1995). Intimacy: Nursing home resident issues and staff training. *The American Journal of Alzheimer's Disease*, March/April.

Hitzig, J. R. & Sprega, M. (1994). Aging, dementia and sexuality. *Proceedings of the International Conference of Alzheimer's International*, Edinburgh.

Hoffman, S. B. & Kaplan, M. (Eds.) (1996). *Special care programs for people with dementia*. Baltimore: Health Professions Press.

Holt, M. G. (1993). Elder abuse in Britain: Meeting the challenge in the 1990s. *Journal of Elder Abuse & Neglect*, 5 (1).

Jorm, A. F. & Henderson, A. S. (1993). *The problem of dementia in Australia* (3rd ed.). Canberra: Department of Health, Housing and Community Services, Aged and Community Care Division.

Kerr, P. E. (1993). *Identification of nurses' stress engendered by caring for dementia residents in nursing homes*. A treatise completed as partial requirement of the Master of Community Health program, Faculty of Health Sciences, The University of Sydney.

Kinsey, A. C., Pomeroy, W. & Martin, C. (1948). *Sexual behaviour in the human male*. Philadelphia: W.B. Saunders.

Kinsey, A.C., Pomeroy, W., Martin, C. & Gebhard, P. M. (1995). *Sexual behaviour in the human female*. Philadelphia: W.B. Saunders.

Koch, S. (1994). Restraining nursing home residents. *Australian Journal of Advanced Nursing*, 11 (2).

Kuhn, D. (1994). The changing face of sexual intimacy in Alzheimer's disease. *American Journal of Alzheimer's Care and Related Disorders and Research*, 9 (5).

Kurrle, S. E., Sadler, P. M. & Cameron, I. D. (1991). Elder abuse: An Australian case series. *The Medical Journal of Australia*, 1 (55).

McCallum, J. (1993). Elder abuse: The 'new' social problem? *Modern Medicine of Australia*, September.

MacFarlane, P. (1995). *Health law, commentary and materials* (2nd ed.). The Federation Press.

Mears, J. (1997). *Triple jeopardy: Gender and abuse of older people*. NSW Advisory Committee on Abuse of Older People, NSW Government Ageing and Disability Department.

Mitchell, K. R., Kerridge, I. H. & Lovat, T. J. (1996). *Bioethics and clinical ethics for health care professionals*. Social Science Press.

Ministerial Taskforce on Psychotropic Medication Use in Nursing Homes (1997). Discussion paper. NSW Health.

Newman, G. & Nichols, C. R. (1960). Sexual activity of men and women between the ages of sixty and ninety-three. *Journal of the American Medical Association*, 173.

NSW Advisory Committee on Abuse of Older People (1995). *Abuse of older people: Inter-agency protocol.*

Office of the Public Guardian of NSW. *Annual Report 1995-96.*

Pfeiffer, E., Verwoerdt, A. & Wang, H. (1968). Sexual behaviour in aged men and women. *Archives of General Psychiatry*, 19.

Public Guardian of NSW. Restraint sometimes proposed to manage grief of elderly. *Bulletin* 2 (2).

Rees, L. & Butel, E. (Eds.) (1985). *Peaks and valleys.* Collins.

Retsas, A. P. (1997). Use of physical restraints in South Australia's nursing homes. *Australian Journal on Ageing*, 16 (4).

Retsas, A. P. & Crabbe, H. (1996). Restraint: Legal implications for aged care. *Australian Journal on Ageing*, 15 (1).

Riggs, A. & Turner, B. S. (1997). The sociology of the postmodern self: Intimacy, identity and emotions in adult life. *Australian Journal on Ageing*, 16 (4).

Riggs, A. (1997). Men, friends and widowhood. *Australian Journal on Ageing*, 16 (4).

Rosewarne, R., Opie, B. A., et al. (1997). Care needs of people with dementia and challenging behaviours living in residential facilities. (Summary Report 1996). In *Aged and Community Care Service Development and Evaluation Reports*, 29. Canberra: Australian Government Printing Service.

Snowdon, J., Miller, R. & Vaughan, R. Behavioural problems in Sydney nursing homes. *International Journal of Geriatric Psychiatry*, 11.

Squires, B., et al. (1995). *Legal issues manual.* NSW Advisory Committee on Abuse of Older People, NSW Government Ageing and Disability Department.

Sherman, B. (1996). Sex? Not my grandmother!. In *Proceedings of Alzheimer's Association of Australia*, 5th National Conference. Brisbane.

Sherman, B. (1994). *Dementia with dignity: A handbook for carers.* Sydney: McGraw Hill.

Sherman, B. (1994). Solving the problem: A planned response to strange and difficult behaviour and disruptive actions. In *Proceedings of Alzheimer's Association of Australia*, 4th National Conference, Sydney.

Sherman, B. (1994). Therapy: Who benefits? A critical evaluation of the routine use of psychological type 'therapy' in dementia programmes. In *Proceedings of the International Conference of Alzheimer's International*, Edinburgh.

Starr, B. D. & Weiner, M. B. (1981). *Sex and sexuality in the mature years.* New York: Stein & Day.

Taylor, W. (1996). Sexuality/Intimacy and how we talk about it. In *Proceedings of Alzheimer's Association of Australia,* 5th National Conference, Brisbane.

Weeks, E. & Sadler, P. (1997). *Elder abuse and dementia.* NSW Advisory Committee on Abuse of Older People, NSW Ageing and Disability Department.

Welander, H. U., Hallberg, I. R. & Axelsson, N. (1995). Nurses' satisfaction with nursing care and work at three care units for severely demented people. *Journal of Psychiatric and Mental Health Nursing, 2.*

Wright, L. K. (1993). *Alzheimer's disease and marriage: An intimate account.* Newbury Park, CA: Sage Publications.

Woolford, H. (1996). Sexuality and sexual counselling for couples, where a partner has dementia. In *Proceedings of Alzheimer's Association of Australia,* 5th National Conference, Brisbane.

Zoblicki, M. (1990). Successful ageing in a public nursing home. In *Proceedings of the 25th Annual Conference of the Australian Association of Gerontology,* Canberra.

Videos

Sexuality and dementia: Carers' perspective (1996). Stirling: Dementia Services Development Centre.

Dementia with dignity (1994). Sydney: Eastway Communications.

A thousand tomorrows: Intimacy, sexuality and Alzheimer's (1995). USA: Terra Nova Films.

Sexuality and dementia (1994). Melbourne: Dementia Services Development Centre.

INDEX